THE COMPLETE Book of Rug Hooking

THE COMPLETE Book
of
Rug
Hooking

SECOND EDITION

By Barbara J. Zarbock

VAN NOSTRAND REINHOLD COMPANY

NEW YORK · TORONTO
LONDON · MELBOURNE

Contents

Illustrations

Foreword: A New Look at an Old Craft

In this book, I hope to introduce you to a permanently exciting and rewarding hobby. Rugmaking is a form of craft work that is pleasurable, profitable and practical, and the technique of hooking is easily and quickly acquired.

I have been making hooked rugs for many years, using various techniques, and ranging from primitive design through traditional and modern patterns. More important, I have worked with all kinds of people, old and young, timid and bold, and have found that the best rugs are created in an atmosphere that allows complete freedom for personal choice in technique, design and color.

So I want to give you an opportunity for self-expression, by presenting a complete picture of all possibilities in the craft. Although I have developed special tastes in design and color, as you will, I offer these as inspiration, not as direction.

There have been many rules of the road laid down in books on rugmaking, but in recent years the road has broadened considerably. I believe the rules are now subject to a freer interpretation than in the past. In fact, there are several roads in the craft, and I wish only to point the way so that you can follow the one that suits you best.

Chapter sub-headings were suggested by questions I have most often been asked about hooking. The ensuing remarks constitute my answer. If you have never hooked, you will find here complete instructions on fundamentals of technique, a discussion, based on personal experience, of available equipment for the present-day craftsman, and suggested approaches to color and design that may prove stimulating and helpful. If you have already made many rugs, I hope to interest you in new aspects of the craft, perhaps enabling you to enlarge your scope.

My fondest wish is that you will sense the pleasure in this hobby, for a hobby should be fun. This one is, as you will discover in it the joys of true self-expression.

I want to express my gratitude to Ruth

Lorenzo of Fairfield, Connecticut, who guided me with skill and patience through the intricacies of realistic shading in hooked rugs. And I owe a real debt to George Wells of Glen Head, Long Island, whose work, teaching and vision have inspired me to explore other areas of the craft.

I am grateful to many suppliers, teachers and individual hookers for constructive advice, information and the loan of rugs to use as illustration. And I am indebted to all the members of my family for their encouragement, to my husband, in particular, for the excellent illustrations in this book, and to Mr. Ward Brackett for the use of his studio for photographic work.

Weston, Connecticut
June, 1961

BARBARA J. ZARBOCK

CHAPTER 1

Rug Hooking for Everyone

Is it Easy to Learn to Hook?

You can learn to hook easily and quickly even though you are not adept at other handwork, such as sewing, embroidery, needlepoint or knitting. Conversely, it is true that the expert needlewoman also finds much satisfaction in hooking.

You will certainly enjoy making hooked rugs, for like most craft work, it fulfills the basic human need to be creative as well as productive. In addition, this craft meets special requirements, as it is a relaxing hobby for busy people and a stimulating one for those who are bored. Since the technique is easy, hooking is a soothing occupation for the harassed housewife or businessman and it can also be enjoyed by children. Because the work requires neither great dexterity nor keen eyesight, it is ideal for elderly people, for convalescents and for the physically handicapped. Finally, rugmaking can be a source of income as well as pleasure.

CREATIVE OPPORTUNITIES

You need not be an artist to choose or draw a good design for a rug and to use color effectively in it. In fact, you may be well prepared already for creative work, as exposure to color and design in many decorative media has formed your tastes and you have practiced selectivity in shopping for clothes and household furnishings. At this moment, you probably have many ideas on design and color and need only sort them out to produce satisfying, artistic results in a rug.

Once you start hooking, you will become increasingly perceptive with regard to color and design. As your awareness develops and your interest in the craft increases, you will begin to translate

1

everything you see into possible use as design or color for a rug.

This hobby will provide unlimited opportunities to use artistic ideas. If you have not dared to be bold in your choice of clothes, it will give you a chance to be lavish with brilliant colors and daring designs in a rug. Or, if you wish, you can explore the delightful possibilities of subtle, soft-hued color schemes. At last, you can express yourself freely, for the best handmade rugs are personal.

PRACTICAL VALUES OF THE CRAFT

This is a practical craft, one that can be enjoyed for remarkably little expense. Indeed, rug hooking is traditionally associated with Yankee thrift, with useful articles produced from scraps of material on hand. A clever craftsman can still use old or inexpensive materials to make a beautiful rug.

The hobby is clean and needs no extensive preparation nor tedious tidying up. You can hook for only a few moments without having to haul out bulky equipment, and you can put your work away quickly if you wish. You can start or abandon the project at any time, not as in many crafts where a particular phase of work must be completed at a sitting.

Rugmaking will fit into almost any home situation, for you can work in a small corner or set up a craft center that will add interest to a room. Since you can give as little or as much time to the hobby as you want, you can fit it into your daily schedule. It is ideal to fill in small segments of time, for most projects can be carried easily. You can hook while waiting for the commuters' train to arrive or for the Scout troop to adjourn. More important, since the work is so absorbing, it can even help to pass those seemingly endless hours of anxiety or sorrow that we must all sometimes get through.

Hooking produces handsome, useful articles for the home. These are durable, besides, for a well-made rug mellows, becoming more attractive with use and time. And hooking is not just a form of busy work. There is special satisfaction in knowing you are making an artistic contribution to the future, not just continuing in the repetitive pattern of so many home endeavors.

Finally, the craft can be profitable and so of real value not only to housewives but also to retired people, to invalids, veterans and those with physical disabilities. Today, there is great demand for durable, handmade articles. Fine hooked work, either rugs or small pieces, such as mats, pillows, chair seats or handbags, brings good prices. Important too is the fact that hooking as a source of income can boost morale as well as a budget.

SPECIAL VALUES OF HOOKING

Hooking is unique among crafts in the special values it offers. First, the work is both stimulating and soothing. The planning period, while color and design are being selected, is exciting, and it is fascinating too to watch the development of your ideas. However, the process of hooking is quiet and peaceful, so you will find both mental and physical relaxation at your rug frame. The work is not so absorbing that it interferes with a desire to think or just to daydream. Nor is it tiring, for hooking requires little physical exertion.

Second, you will experience the joys of sharing, for rugmaking is a form of self-expression that can happily include others. In the process, you will not "lose" your hobby, for since there is such wide choice in technique and color, your rug can always reflect your own personality. In fact, I have seen many examples of the same design hooked by different persons and if free choice of color and technique has been exercised, the results resemble each other only slightly.

Your family will certainly want to share your hobby. Their suggestions for design and color can be helpful, and may initiate the plan for a rug. It is even possible for various members of a family to work on the same rug, since hooking is something almost everyone can do. Your friends will be interested and may want to learn how to hook. Both family and friends will undoubtedly broadcast the news of your hobby and be eager to bring others to see the project on which you are working.

Finally, and best of all, hooking is fun. You will cherish each moment you can spend with this work. Your pleasure in a craft in which you can express yourself so fully will be reflected within the family as well as outside.

RUGMAKERS GET TOGETHER

While hooking is well suited to solitude, it is also excellent for a group. If previously you have found it distressing to work in a group, I think you will note a difference in rugmaking gatherings. Everyone is getting something done,

learning something, and having a good time socializing with other hookers. A free exchange of ideas is characteristic of these get-togethers, and it is common practice to offer help in the form of material as well as praise and constructive advice. A hooking friend may well give you the shirt off her back if it is a color you need.

Since the hobby attracts all kinds of people, many hooking groups are composed of women of different ages, interests and backgrounds. I have found special pleasure in working in such a mixed gathering, for the range of conversation is usually broad and the atmosphere gay and kindly. Inevitably your own horizons are extended and your sympathies increased. Friendships thrive in this climate, friendships that are much cherished and tend to last forever.

AN ENDLESSLY EXCITING CRAFT

Have you already tried several crafts, going through the learning process, buying equipment and arranging other activities to accomodate a hobby, only to end up with a single finished, or half-finished product and no further interest? Rest assured that hooking is endlessly exciting. Once you start on a rug, your mind will be flooded with ideas for more rugs, rugs you can hardly wait to start. Always, the promise of the rug-to-be will carry you quickly through the one on which you are working.

Indeed your only problem may be to keep from starting several rugs at the same time. I am always ahead of the present project with new ideas for designs and colors. While I try not to start another rug until the present one is at least half finished, I confess I do not always succeed in this effort of will.

MORE THAN JUST A HOBBY

The craft for you, as for me, can be more than just a hobby. My husband, who should know, has flippantly but perhaps truly described it as "a way of life." After you start hooking, you, too, may find the days too short to encompass all your ideas for rugs. Soon you will keep a note pad on your bedside table for late-hour sketching of designs, and you will rise early to try out a new color on your pattern. Even if scientists say it cannot be done, you will dream, as I do, in color.

Eventually, you will keep extra hooks in convenient places. You will examine the texture and color of clothes you buy, and those your friends, and strangers, are wearing, with an eye to their possible use in rugs. Thus you will enter the world of the rug hooker, where you manage somehow to do all that you must more quickly in order to have time to hook.

CHAPTER 2

Hooked Rugs of the Past

When and Where Did Rug Hooking Start?

Hooking is such an ancient skill, the beginnings so lost in antiquity, that authorities differ on date of origin. However, it is well established that the technique was used in Europe long before it appeared in America.

EUROPEAN ORIGINS

It is known that hooked fabrics were made in Egypt as early as the fifth century, A.D. and that the skill spread from there into Spain, and from Spain to France. In the Scandinavian countries, the technique may have developed independently, for it also appeared there hundreds of years ago. William Winthrop Kent, in his book *The Hooked Rug*, says that he has seen examples in the Oslo Museum in Norway of hooked garments or coverlets made by Viking families of the Bronze Age.

The knowledge of hooking was probably brought by Scandinavian invaders from Europe to the British Isles. However, it is possible that special circumstances in sections of England may have produced an independent discovery of the skill there also.

By the beginning of the nineteenth century, there were weaving industries in most parts of England. Weaving was done mainly in the workers' homes and bits of yarn left over from the process were usually considered to belong to the individual weaver. These short ends of yarn were called "thrums." With the knowledge of weaving to provide a foundation fabric and the readily-available thrums, it was a natural step to the invention of a combined use for these materials.

The result was a way of making rugs called "thrumming." A long needle was bent at one end to make a hooked tool

5

with which to draw the ends of yarn up through a woven backing. Then the surface was sheared, in part or in its entirety, according to the preference of the worker. It is interesting to note that tools and methods used today in rugmaking are basically the same as these.

THE FIRST HOOKED RUGS IN AMERICA

Hooked rugs in America were first made in coastal areas, where the craft was introduced by sailors and settlers from both continental Europe and Britain. Many of the early rugs show ancestral influence. Those made in the Middle Atlantic States often included Dutch landscape scenes and reflected color styles then popular in Holland. Contemporary English ideas in color and decoration appeared in rugs made in New England and in Virginia, and hooked work in Nova Scotia and Quebec frequently imitated the elaborate scrolls and floral designs of French Aubusson carpets.

In the new country, special circumstances combined to give an impetus to hooking. Necessity was one, as the technique could be used in making bed covers for warmth, and rugs to keep the chill off dirt or board floors. Another was frugality, an essential trait in early settlers, for hooking provided a use for material too worn to serve any other purpose. Finally, there was a longing for beauty, inherent in all people and especially important to the immigrants, who had brought only the essentials of living with them from their native lands. Housewives even swept or drew designs in the sand or dirt floor of their cabins in an effort to provide some small decoration. Any chance to create

beauty was appealing, and hooked rugs offered this both in color and design.

Certain qualities on which we still pride ourselves as a nation also helped to advance the craft. A spirit of independence caused rugmakers to move rapidly from imitation of the art concepts of their separate homelands to a development of their own ideas. An adventurous outlook brought fresh designs. A lively imagination produced rugs that freely combined factual knowledge with individual fancy, and industry kept hookers at work despite paucity of material. Determination and ingenuity produced the tools for rug-work, hooks fashioned of wood, bone and nails, like those shown in Illustration 1.

CHARACTERISTICS OF ANTIQUE RUGS

All antique rugs have sentimental value today, but certain ones have characteristics that make them artistic heirlooms as well. Colors are effective because only a few are used in a single rug. Restricted use of color probably resulted from the fact that the materials for making dyes, such as roots, bark, flowers, and berries, had to be laboriously collected and then carefully distilled for use. Early designs, like early color schemes, are simple and bold, the result of a drawing done at home by an untutored artist. In addition, care in planning, natural artistry in design and color, and meticulous workmanship are apparent in a number of old rugs.

It seems that limiting circumstances, lack of commercial patterns and dyes, actually contributed to the beauty of many antique rugs. However, most early hookers were hampered by these circumstances and also by inadequate equipment, scarcity of material and lack of education in design, color, and technique. Furthermore, in early times hooking was usually intended to serve a practical purpose; design and color were secondary.

As a result, antique rugs are not all of equal artistic merit, from the standpoint of design, color, or workmanship. In some,

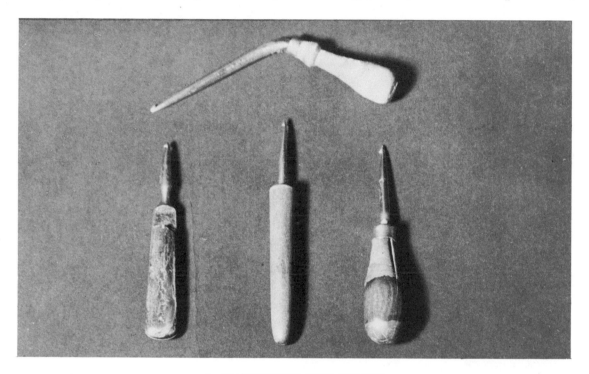

1. HANDMADE RUG HOOKS

From Olive B. Russell's Collection

These tools are all more than one hundred years old. Carefully fashioned of wood and hand-wrought nails, they have been passed down from one generation of rugmakers to another.

designs are haphazard and workmanship crude. In others, clash of color is distressing still, even after years of mellowing.

THEMES IN AMERICAN DESIGN

For their designs, early American rugmakers chose themes from several areas of their daily experience. Floral rugs were the most popular, with patterns ranging from rather intricate bouquets to a few primitive posies.

Marine rugs were common, many being hooked by sailors during long whaling voyages. Traditionally, it was not thought effeminate for seamen to do this work. Women also used marine symbols in rugs. Full-rigged ships were a favorite motif, as well as anchors, tridents, ropes and waves.

Scenic designs were frequent, usually with trees, houses, churches, barns, and people drawn as authentically as the sketcher's talent permitted. Aside from the appeal of their quaintness, these rugs are valued as documentary material on life in the country and in the towns of early America.

Animal patterns were often hooked, for farm animals and house pets were available as models and relatively easy to draw. Wild creatures, too, were plentiful, to inspire rugs like *The Reindeer,* Illustration 2.

As national pride developed, patriotic designs appeared, with drawings commemorating historic events in the new country and eagles and flags as decorative motifs. At the same time, mottoes were sometimes incorporated into a pattern, such time-honored ones as "Home Sweet Home" and "God Bless Our Home."

2. THE REINDEER
30 by 52 inches

Date and Origin Unknown   *Owned by Mr. and Mrs. Richard May*

In this delightful example of an early animal design, the startled deer is hooked in deep red and gold on a warm gray background. The primitive scroll is in red, and the border, probably once solid black, has mellowed to a lovely, antique green-black hue.

RISE AND FALL OF THE CRAFT

Interest in rug hooking increased progressively in America, eventually reaching a peak during the Civil War period, when the technique was familiar to people in all the northern colonies and many rugs were made durable enough to be passed on from one generation to the next. However, as yet nothing had been done to improve equipment for rug-makers, or to provide help in design and color. It was Edward Frost, a veteran of the War Between the States, who gave the craft its greatest impetus by producing stamped patterns for rugs.

Soon after the war, Frost returned to his home in Biddeford, Maine, and invested his savings in a variety of dry goods and household utensils which he peddled from door to door throughout New England. He traveled through Maine, Massachusetts, New Hampshire, and Vermont, bartering as well as selling. Often, he exchanged his wares for a hooked rug or for a pattern drawn by one of the housewives on his route. The demand of successive customers for copies of these designs and for new ones prompted him to devise a way of printing patterns. He perfected a stencil for this purpose and eventually worked out a process for printing in color. His business flourished, and he drew many designs himself to add to those he had collected.

Because of Frost's commercial patterns, rugmaking was introduced to a broad area and many more people became involved in the craft. But, his designs were not all artistic and, unfortunately, their advent resulted in a decline in original work. Even though much rug-work was done, the period that followed was an arid one from an artistic standpoint, with few expressions of individual taste and talent.

During the late nineteenth and early twentieth centuries, several individuals in New England recognized the need to improve standards in the craft. They succeeded in interesting others and this resulted in an arts-and-crafts movement that brought fresh talent and skill to rug-work, provided education in technique, design, and color and produced a variety of patterns artistically conceived and drawn. The appeal of new designs drew people to the craft and qualified teachers were provided for the growing number of beginners. There followed a period of intense interest and productivity in hooking, one that was characterized by high craft standards.

The craft was destined to suffer a decline once more, however, when twentieth-century American industrialization began to produce a quantity of machine-made articles. As general interest in assembly-line products increased, the value of handmade things declined. There seemed little advantage in tedious, slow work as opposed to a rapid, easy method.

A NEW ERA ARRIVES

In recent years, a new era in crafts has arrived as people have become disenchanted with the products, pace and values of a machine age. The longing for beauty and the need to create it are reasserting themselves. Fine, imaginative, one-of-a-kind articles are newly appreciated, and patient, careful workmanship is again considered praiseworthy. As a result, rug hooking is attracting more and more people, thoughtful people who want to express their love of beauty in an individual, creative way.

CHAPTER 3

Rugmaking Today

What Kind of Hooked Rug Shall I Make?

ODAY, a craftsman is not limited by lack of materials, dyes, equipment or information, and so has free choice as to the kind of hooked rug to make. There are numerous, artistic commercial designs from which to choose, and many sources of information to help you if you wish to draw your own pattern.

Pamphlets and books are devoted to advice on technique and color-planning. With the special dyes now available, you can obtain almost any conceivable color or shade. By selecting from an abundant supply of different materials, you can achieve variety in texture. Finally, you can choose from different kinds of backing, tools and equipment for your rugwork.

DECIDING THE KIND OF RUG TO MAKE

While the present day hooker has a great advantage over her predecessors in freedom of selection, such unlimited choice can be bewildering, especially for a beginner. Therefore, to aid decision on the kind of rug to make, I suggest you consider these three essentials: first, the size and shape rug best suited to a selected location; second, suitability of a design to this setting and finally, the total effect of a special design, technique or color scheme.

THE IMPORTANCE OF SIZE

One reason why the size of a rug is important is that once this has been decided it will be easier to select design and to plan color. A good way to determine the best size is to select the place where a rug will be used. To suit the location, a rug should be large enough to fill the area adequately. But a hooked rug need not imitate wall-to-wall carpeting, for its decorative effect is enhanced by a certain amount of surrounding floor surface.

On the other hand, a rug that is skimpy will always look forlorn. In making a hooked rug, you save only a little time with a small one that you can finish quickly. If it is too small for a chosen spot, the valuable hours of work are partially wasted.

After choosing the place, use wrapping paper to help you figure out the proper size for your rug. Lay the paper on the floor and cut or fold it to the proportions that look best. Then either draw a design or buy a commercial pattern to fit the size. Of course, you cannot always decide on size by choosing location. You may

have many possible places for a hooked rug and yet find it hard to settle on one area. Or perhaps you have no place for a rug at the moment, but still want to make one.

In either case, psychological factors may help you decide on size. If you tend to be discouraged by a large project, are perhaps inclined to abandon work at the halfway point, it is probably best for you to make a small rug. A small one can be finished rather quickly and will give you the boost that accompanies completion. On the other hand, you may attach little importance to a small project and so be inclined to neglect it. Perhaps you respond to the challenge of a large en-

3. EAGLE WELCOME
30 by 46 inches

Designed and hooked by the author

The eagle is a favorite motif, one that can be used in either a modern or traditional setting. This decorative entry rug has a gray-green background, an eagle in shades of gray, gold lettering and touches of antique black in the border and the central motif.

deavor. If so, go ahead and plan a big rug.

From my viewpoint, there is no right or wrong size for either a novice or an expert. Hooking is not necessarily a progression from small articles to large ones. Some people never want to make a room-sized rug, while others are not content until they do. The essential thing, when deciding on size, is to "know thyself."

A VARIETY OF SHAPES

The shape of a rug, as well as the size, is important in a decorative scheme. Here too you can make a decision by selecting the location and cutting or folding paper to a shape that looks right. Generally, a rectangular rug is the most useful as it will fit various places, as hallways, entries or focal points in a room. An oval is almost equally adaptable and graceful as well. A half-round rug (Illustration 3) is well suited to entries and, although traditionally used in front of doors opening outside, this shape is also charming for interior doorways. A circular pattern is handsome, either as a room-sized rug or as a small one to use beside a bed or other piece of furniture, in front of a fireplace or in an entry. However, a large, circular rug is somewhat difficult to place effectively for you will want the circumference to be visible, not concealed by encroaching furniture. Finally, a square rug may be just right for a special place even though this shape does not adapt readily to many locations.

These are the basic shapes. Of course, it is possible to have variations of them. But if you are not deciding shape on the basis of location, choose a rectangular or oval pattern. Either can be fitted easily into different places.

TIME TO HOOK

A frequent question from a beginner is, "How much time does it take to make a hooked rug?" Presumably, the decision on size will be based on the reply.

The only answer I can give is that your attitude toward a rug will determine the amount of time it takes to complete it. Whether you have much spare time or just a few free moments a day, the time you spend hooking will depend largely on your interest in the project. For this reason, the best guarantee of finishing a rug quickly is to have a strong, personal feeling about a design and the colors to be used in it.

It is true that a pattern of large areas can be hooked faster than one of intricate, small sections that require slower, more careful work. But, filling big sections is far less interesting than working out a number of small areas. Also, using only one or two colors becomes boring, while a frequent change of color is stimulating.

For me, the time it takes to complete a rug certainly depends on the excitement I feel about design and color. For example: I finished *Summertime*, a 30- by 45-inch rug (Color Plate XIV) in just two weeks, as I enjoyed the chance to change color and hook the various motifs. For the same reasons, I completed a much larger project, the stair carpet called *Parade of Seasons* (Illustration 4), in six months, quite a short time for a rug of such size.

On the other hand, it took me over a year to finish *The Sampler* (Illustration

4. PARADE OF THE SEASONS

Designed and hooked by the author

This stair carpet follows a theme, using birds as motifs to show the progress of the seasons, from spring to fall. First comes the chickadee, while snow still flies. Summer begins with an oriole amid golden meadow flowers. The rug and the season end four steps beyond, with a riser depicting a towhee on autumn leaves. A geometric design was used on the treads for practical reasons; it does not show wear and soil readily and is a good way to use up leftover pieces of material. (Photograph by Bill Margerin. Courtesy *Living for Young Homemakers*.)

5). This rug, in shades of only one color with repeated motifs became uninteresting after one small section was completed. As a result, I worked on it sporadically and abandoned it altogether for long periods. It required real determination to finish it at all, and frequent "vacations" when I hooked more interesting designs.

Since the time it takes to make a hooked rug depends so much on design, be sure to select a pattern you find exciting, one on which you can have fun with color, one you can hardly wait to start and will be eager to hook to the finished result. Undoubtedly, you will bring your best efforts to such a project, working when you are most alert and untired. Indeed, you may find more time to hook than you now think you can spare. This will be insurance of a fine, finished rug.

SELECTING A DESIGN

Pleasure in the craft really begins with choice of design. You may have discovered this already by considering a pattern you plan to draw yourself. Working on an original design is most interesting, and you will find helpful advice in Chapter 4 to encourage your efforts in this direction.

Perhaps you would rather choose a design from the many offered commercially. Among these, you may find one that is so appealing that you decide to throw considerations of size and shape to the winds, selecting a pattern because it is irresistible. While one selected on these grounds may not suit a special location, fortunately for hookers, most

patterns can be made to fit various settings through judicious use of color.

However, no matter how you decide on a design, it is important to realize that there are two basic types. One is a one-way design, a drawing that is best viewed from one side only, and so well suited to entries, halls, stairs or in front of furniture or other focal points. Examples of this kind are *Threshold Rug* in Figure 6, *Primrose Path* in Figure 7 and *Setting Hen* in Figure 3. The other kind of design is all-direction, a drawing that can be viewed equally well from all sides. Examples of this are *Beginner's Luck* in Figure 1, *September Song* in Figure 2 and *Sunburst* in Figure 8. This type can be used in any location.

THE EFFECT OF A HOOKED RUG

A final, important consideration is the effect of design, color and texture. A hooked rug can have more decorative impact than any other element in a room. Indeed, as a rug is usually the first furnishing in a house to attract attention, it tends to set the tone of its surroundings. You will therefore be wise to decide in advance what effect you want.

You can plan a rug to contrast or blend with a setting. Usually one of luxurious texture and elaborate pattern looks well in a formal room, while a less intricate design of muted hue and incon-spicuous texture suits an informal home. A primitive design in rich, warm colors offers effective contrast to contemporary furniture, a modern, bold pattern makes an interesting foil for the delicate workmanship of much antique furniture.

As hooked rugs in themselves have character, you can suit the mood of a home, creating a cozy, intimate feeling with warm colors and early designs, a cool, elegant mood with a realistic pattern in soft, subtle hues, or an exciting effect with a bold design of brilliant color or unusual texture. A mood need not be serious either. A touch of whimsey in a rug can be a delightful personal note for your home.

CHOICE OF COMMERCIAL DESIGNS

Commercial designs for rugs, sold as patterns printed on backing, are of many kinds and subjects. You can buy designs adapted from Early American hooked work or patterns inspired by the rugs of Europe and the Orient. You can purchase formal, quaint, abstract, or whimsical designs, and flower, fruit, animal, scenic, or geometric motifs. Furthermore, you can choose between simple, stylized drawings and intricate, realistic ones.

The designs shown here illustrate the range of commercial patterns, and there are many designers besides those repre-

5. THE SAMPLER
2 feet 8 inches by 7 feet

Designed and hooked by the author

The mottoes, stylized motifs and border of this design were adapted from a needlework sampler of the early 1800's. The rug is hooked in shades of one color, from pale pink to deep terra cotta.

FIG. 1

FIG. 2

Figure 1. BEGINNER'S LUCK

Mrs. Harry King Design   *30 by 40 inches*

This graceful, small oval with its delicate, loose arrangement of garden flowers is especially suited to warm rosy hues, dusty blues and soft, spring greens.

Figure 2. SEPTEMBER SONG

Pearl McGown Design   *29 by 43 inches*

This handsome, rather formal design would be equally effective in rich purple, green and muted golds or in cool blue, gray-green and pale yellows, and it would be exquisite in any setting.

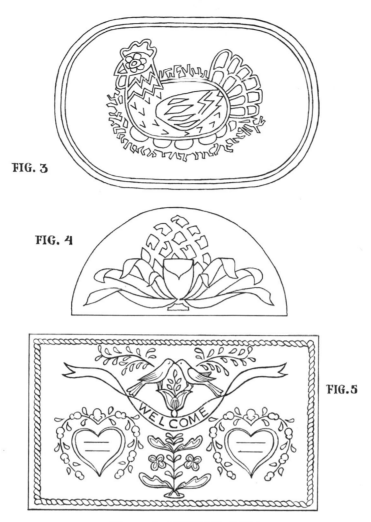

FIG. 3

FIG. 4

FIG. 5

Figure 3. SETTING HEN

Dolli Tingle Design   *30 by 40 inches*

This design could be worked as a modern or a primitive rug. In brilliant hues of gold and scarlet with accents of black, it would be a sophisticated touch in a modern room.

Figure 4. PINEAPPLE

George Wells Design   *18 by 36 inches*

This half-round uses a classic symbol of hospitality, the pineapple; it would be effective in three colors, perhaps warm beige, deep brown-greens, and golds.

Figure 5. ANNIVERSARY

E. Dana Design   *30 by 50 inches*

This charming design would provide a gay touch for an entry whether hooked in brilliant reds, blues, and yellows or in antiqued hues of brown-red, gold, and faded blues.

FIG. 6

FIG. 7

FIG. 8

Figure 6. THRESHOLD RUG

Hall-Prescott-Burnham Design   *24 by 40 inches—No. 2-r*

A graceful composition of stylized flowers, this design could be worked as a
striking modern rug or a quaint primitive piece.

Figure 7. PRIMROSE PATH

Margaret Leslie Design   *30 by 73 inches*

This delightful design would be perfect for a hallway, in light, bright, cool
pastels. Give the stepping stones an appearance of solidity by using deep, warm
grays and add a touch of brilliance in color of the bird.

Figure 8. SUNBURST

Dolli Tingle Design   *3 by 4 feet, 6 inches*

The boldness and simplicity of this design are retained by using just a few
colors, butter yellow for the center of the sunburst, greenish yellow for the
rays, olive green for the background, accented with touches of deep brown-
green or black.

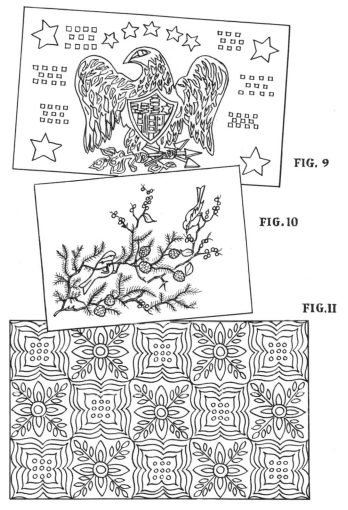

FIG. 10

FIG. 11

Figure 9. FOUR STAR EAGLE

George Wells Design   *3 feet, 6 inches by 5 feet, 6 inches*

The clean lines and beautiful balance of motifs make this design suitable for either a modern or a primitive rug, to be worked in solid, brilliant hues or in mottled, muted colors.

Figure 10. CHICKADEES

Margaret McKenzie Design   *2 by 3 feet*

This appealing design would be attractive in crisp black and white on a warm gray background, with rich greens and browns in pine needles and cones and a touch of brilliant scarlet in the berries.

Figure 11. PEMBROKE

Karlkraft Design   *29 by 47 inches*

This delicate geometric would be lovely in powder blues and off-whites, with touches of warm rose. It would be effective also as a modern rug in clear, yellows, greens, or reds with accents of black.

6. BOUQUET
26 by 35 inches

Designed and hooked by the author

This pattern was adapted from a commercial design and it is my first hooked rug, made fifteen years ago. I used three gray flannel skirts for the background, a darker gray skirt for the inner border and a black skirt for the outer border and the stems. Scraps of cotton, wool and jersey were used for the flowers and leaves. All material was hand cut, the pattern was mounted on an old picture frame and the rug was completed for less than two dollars, including cost of the hand hook and the burlap backing.

sented. In addition, all those whose work is shown have many patterns, of various types, beside those illustrated. Designers of rugs have catalogues with descriptions of the patterns they sell. I suggest you send for several catalogues before you select your pattern. Even if you plan to draw your own design, it is helpful to see what others have done. (Suppliers are listed at the end of this book.)

As you look at these designs, think about color. In descriptions with the illustrations, I have suggested colors that have occurred to me, but these are intended only as inspiration. They are not necessarily the only color for a pattern. Try to imagine working each of these rugs in colors that you like, colors that will give the desired effect in your home.

CHAPTER 4

Original Designs

Can I Draw My Own Design for a Rug?

Y ou will enjoy the craft most if you take advantage of the many creative opportunities it offers. Designing is one of the most important of these, since it gives you a chance to develop your own pictorial ideas. Furthermore, hooking will enable you to develop your ideas in your own way.

Designing for rugs is not difficult. Indeed, it is an ideal art field in which to begin drawing, even though you have never sketched before. Of course, if you have had art training, you will use your knowledge to draw a pattern for your rug.

A GOOD APPROACH TO DESIGNING

It is important to adopt a liberal approach toward original work for a desire to create and a willingness to try to create will help you over the first hurdles. Do not be intimidated by the word "art."

True art is basically within the ability of us all. As the essence of art is communication, the idea for a drawing is more important than the lines. And because a design conveys an idea, a good idea, well-conceived and well-executed will make an artistic rug.

Do not belittle your efforts to draw. The design of rugs is now a recognized art form, and the beauty of a rug is considered important, not secondary to its practical purpose, as in the past. Design contributes the essential beauty to a rug and is usually its most striking feature.

Determine to make a start, for as you begin to create, you will find both your hand skill and your powers of observation increasing. Practice observation, keep a notebook of ideas for designs and try to translate these into sketches. Even a few lines that will serve to fasten an idea in your memory can be developed later into a pattern for a rug. At the start this may seem like hard work, but you will soon discover that these attempts will increase your perception and sensitivity to many forms of art.

Exercise judgment, for taste is essential to good design. Since fashions in design are fleeting, particularly so in rugs, plan a pattern that is fundamentally attractive. You need not be restricted to the usual rug design, but do beware of what is intentionally bizarre or extremely comic, for these effects are soon dated.

Above all, try for originality. Copying anything in its entirety is no guarantee of good design. Though you may borrow from patterns that please you, depend on your knowledge and imagination to make an individual composition, one that will convey your own idea.

THE BASIS OF DESIGN

Your first venture in drawing will be easier if you understand a few principles of design and then apply them to your work. Composition, dominance, and simplicity are three terms that describe the basis of design.

Composition refers to the arrangement of shapes in space; it involves balance, an equalizing of area with the amount of drawing. In design for a rug, composition is limited to arranging shapes or groupings on a single plane, the surface of the rug. The area is prescribed by the size of the rug.

There are a number of standard compositions. Each one is illustrated in this chapter by an original design. A favorite is a single figure or group centered on a background, as in *Weathervane Horse*,

Illustration 7. In this design, the large central figure is balanced by a proportionate amount of background area. *MG*, Illustration 8, is basically the same type, although in this rug the figure covers almost the whole surface.

Another composition places motifs around the background area in a balance of sizes, as in *Sleeping Cats*, Illustration 9. In this rug, the large central figures are balanced by a narrow, curving band of related motifs. *Noah's Ark*, Color Plate VII, is the same type, with a careful balance of numerous, varied-size shapes.

Always popular is a composition like *Flower Fancy*, Color Plate VI. Although this appears to be a free, scattered design, it is actually a carefully balanced arrangement of weights and sizes of motifs.

You are sure to like the repeat, a design of the same or similar figures placed in definite order on a background. *Ring Around the Rosy*, Color Plate X, is an imaginative composition of this kind. *The Sampler*, Illustration 5, is also essentially a repeat, with letters and stylized motifs used over and over. A repeat design is probably the easiest for a beginner. Anything can be repeated: geometric forms, as circles, crosses, diamonds and squares; natural shapes, as leaves, ferns and flowers; or stylized motifs like the dancing children. For this type of pattern, you need only draw a figure and then repeat it in ordered fashion on the background. It is easy to work out such a design, and you can vary the effect just by changing the color of the repeats.

The second element of good design is dominance. To obtain this, make your design large enough to be forceful and

7. WEATHERVANE HORSE
28 by 40 inches

Designed and hooked by Jean Mercier and her nine-year-old daughter, Madeleine

The sprightly horse in this design was inspired by an old weathervane, and an old black coat was used to hook it. The background, of variegated green-beiges, was made of two old camel's-hair coats, bleached and then tinted with color. Two elements add interest to the design: the straight rows of hooking in the background, and the fact that Mother hooked one half of the rug and her young daughter the other half.

easily seen from a distance. You can feature, or give dominance, to one aspect of your design by setting it off with plenty of clear background around it. In other words, give it room to breathe, making sure it is not hidden by subordinate detail.

The keynote of good design is simplicity, so do not overload a pattern in a mistaken effort to be artistic. Whether a rug is to be modern or traditional, plan only the amount of design necessary to convey your idea. For an individual, sincere appearance, work directly from what you actually know and feel.

Generally a design of a few strong lines is successful in a rug. Such a drawing is easier for a new rugmaker who must be concerned with learning several aspects

8. MG
28 by 62 inches
(not including frame)

Designed and hooked by James P. McCleery

Jim has used one hobby to immortalize another in this decorative framed picture of his favorite racing car. This is a typical man's design with strong lines and bold colors. Lower part of the background is beige, the upper part black, the bisecting band is aqua and the MG bright red, with touches of beige and black.

IDEAS FOR PATTERNS

There are innumerable sources for ideas that will help you with your own pattern for a rug. One of the best is design as it appears in both historic and contemporary rugs. Study rugs pictured in books on rugmaking, in magazine articles and in the catalogues of designers. Visit galleries and museums to see the designs in old rugs and, whenever possible, go to rug shows and to the studios of designers so you will be aware of the patterns being used today. It is standard procedure to derive ideas from other craftsmen, and this need not affect the complete honesty and originality of your own work.

Nature provides another source of inspiration. Flowers are so often the basis for rug designs that they are commonly associated with hooked work. Flowers can be stylized, as in *Flower Fancy*, Color Plate VI, or realistic, as in *Woodland*, Color Plate I.

However, you are not limited to saying it with flowers, for animals, birds, insects or fish also offer good motifs. The forms of mountains, lakes, trees, branches and leaves, the patterns of clouds and waves, the shapes and markings of stones, shells and snowflakes—all these, and countless other natural forms, can be

of the craft at the same time, namely technique and the use of color and texture as well as design.

adapted for use either in abstract or realistic designs.

In fact, all decorative crafts are sources of inspiration for rugs. Different kinds of needlework, such as embroidery, needlepoint, crewel work and appliqué offer distinctive motifs. *American Fancy*, Color Plate XXII, is an example of a rug design adapted from needlework. Textile designs, often by talented artists, also provide ideas for pattern and color. Decorations on china and glass, on Delftware, Willoware, Staffordshire china and Sandwich glass, for instance, can suggest motifs. Woodwork, stonework, metalwork, ceramics and mosaics, all used for centuries for decorative purposes, are an excellent source of ideas. Patterns on wallpaper, old valentines, greeting cards and decorated boxes, on manuscripts and old books, charts and maps, can also supply a motif for your rug.

Indeed, a study of many forms of art will help you in drawing a design for your rug. Paintings are fine sources of ideas, both in subject and composition. Even children's drawings, usually so fresh and gay, may suggest designs for rugs (Illustration 10).

It is likely that you will select and adapt motifs from several sources before completing your design. Once again, try to combine motifs in an original, imaginative way that will convey your own idea.

PUTTING DESIGN ON RUG BACKING

When you have decided on main ideas and perhaps chosen supporting motifs, you are ready to put your design on rug backing. There are several ways to do this. Use the one easiest for you.

First, define the size and shape of the rug by marking an outline on the backing. Use an indelible pencil for this, like the *Magic Marker* in Illustration 14. Leave at least 2 inches of material beyond the outline to turn back for binding or hemming the finished rug.

USING CUT-OUTS

One satisfactory way to put design on backing is to use cut-outs. Cut rough shapes out of paper, using lightweight cardboard or construction paper. Arrange these cut-out forms on the backing within the rug outline until you have a well-balanced composition. Then remove the cut-outs, one at a time, and trim them to final shapes. As you complete each one, pin it in place and draw around it with your marking pencil. After main motifs are drawn, it will be easy to add details freehand. *Flower Fancy*, Color Plate VI, is a good example of a design done with cut-

9. SLEEPING CATS
27 by 38 inches

Designed by Garrett Price   *Hooked by Florence Price*

This design, by a well-known cartoonist, is a charming portrayal of beloved pets. Mrs. Price hooked the background in warm, pinky-brown, the cats in gray, tan, and white, the fish in gray, tan, and green and the balls in green and yellow. Touches of black define and accentuate the motifs.

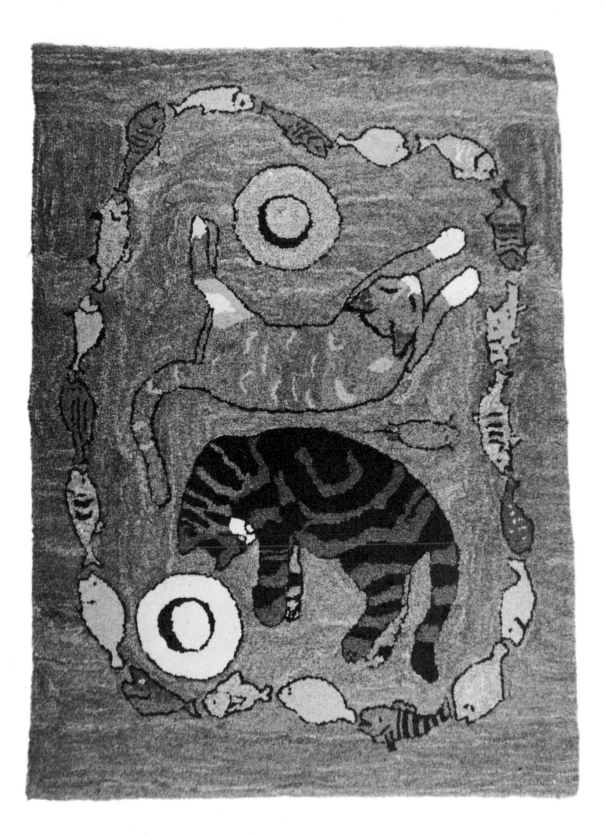

10. KITTY
20 by 24 inches

Designed and hooked by Sarah Zarbock at age 10

This smiling, winsome cat is a good example of the appealing quality of children's drawings. The design was small enough to be finished quickly, and it was fun to make, in gray and black tweed with touches of pink in the ears and tongue and gold in the eyes.

11. SKI SILHOUETTE
36 by 41 inches

Designed and hooked by Hans Vierling

This design shows how simplicity in both motifs and color treatment can make
an effective rug. Done in just black and white, it achieves a two-dimensional
feeling through reduced size of the figures in the background and through use
of a few bisecting lines. The various postures of the figures are authentic to
the sport of skiing, as would be expected since Hans has seven children who
are winter sports enthusiasts.

outs. *Ski Silhouette,* Illustration 11, also shows how cut-outs can make a pattern.

It is fun to experiment with cut-outs and in the process you may make an unexpected, interesting pattern. Fold paper to get geometric shapes, cut folded paper for openwork effects or cut random curls of paper to spread out on backing for a free, swirling design.

DRAWING AND TRACING

If your design is not suited to cut-outs, drawing and tracing may be the best method for you. Since it is easier for most people to make a relatively small sketch, I suggest you draw your design on a small piece of paper first. An 8- by 11-inch sheet of graph paper is excellent, since it is ruled off in small, even squares making it easy to enlarge the pattern to the size you want.

After drawing the design on graph paper, enlarge it on paper the size of the rug or draw it directly on the backing. To enlarge on the backing, mark on this fabric the same number of squares covered by your drawing on graph paper. The squares should be even and large enough to cover the surface of the rug. Then, draw the lines in each of these large squares exactly as you drew them on the small squares of your sketch.

Follow the same procedure to enlarge a small drawing for a large sheet of paper. Then this can be transferred to backing by placing carbon paper between the sketch and the foundation fabric. Extra large sheets of carbon paper can be purchased at art-supply stores.

To transfer the drawing at one time, fasten the backing securely to a table or to the floor with thumbtacks. Spread the carbon paper over the backing, then tack the paper pattern on top. Use a blunt pencil or an orangewood stick to go over the lines of the drawing. Bear down heavily, so that the markings will come through clearly on the backing. After removing the paper pattern and carbon, immediately remark any lines that are faint. Use an indelible marking pencil for this.

If it is easier for you to transfer small sections of a design, rather than the whole pattern at once, pin a small sheet of carbon paper under the section to be traced. Follow the same procedure until you have traced all the separate parts of the design.

PERFORATED PATTERNS

Instead of using carbon paper to transfer the design to the backing, you can make a perforated pattern. First draw your design on a sheet of stiff heavy paper the size of the rug. Then punch small holes all along the lines of the drawing. You can use a commercial perforating wheel, available at art-supply stores, or a straight pin or needle.

Pin the perforated design to the backing and with a crayon, dark-colored chalk or an indelible marking pencil, draw heavily across the punched holes. Lines will thus appear on the backing as a series of closely-set dots. After removing the perforated pattern, you can join these dots into a continuous line.

FREEHAND DRAWING

The easiest way to put a design on backing is to draw it freehand directly on the fabric. This method is fun, too, and though it may require courage, it does tend to insure a loose, unhibited line well suited to a rug design.

For freehand sketching, stretch your foundation fabric tight, either on a frame or with tacks on table or floor. Then use a heavy crayon or marking pencil and draw the main design with bold strokes. Work in the less important details afterward. Or you can paint the design on backing, with a mixture of dye and water applied with a small, stiff-bristled brush. Try for effects of shadow and washes of color that will be interesting to translate into material when you start hooking.

ALL ABOUT BORDERS

Most pictures look best when framed, but this is not always true of the design in hooked rugs. Therefore, when putting a pattern on backing, let the border go until last. This will keep you from limiting a composition right at the beginning, and from framing a design that may not require it.

A drawing that is not bordered tends to be projected or emphasized, as you can see in *Weathervane Horse*, Illustration 7. A design that is framed tends to be drawn back or played down by the border, as in *Family Tree*, Color Plate IV.

However, if a border suits your design and contributes something to it, then by all means have one. But plan it carefully to get the effect you want. Generally speaking, a wide border is suitable for a bold design and a narrow border for a delicate pattern. Intensity of color in a border or detailed design within it will give an illusion of width.

CHAPTER 5

Materials for Rug-Work

What Materials are Best for Hooking?

ALMOST any material can be employed for rugs, but some kinds are easier to hook than others. And some fabrics are better suited to certain methods, to particular kinds of patterns or for rugs to be used in special locations. The material contributes both to the practical and aesthetic success of a hooked rug. Therefore, you should consider fabrics in direct relation to their suitability.

PRACTICAL MATERIAL

To be practical, material for a rug should be durable, inexpensive, readily available and easy to hook.

It is especially important to use durable material, for the wearing quality of a rug depends to a great extent on the strength of the fabric. On any rug you make you will expend thought, energy, and time and you will therefore want it to last. For a rug in an area of heavy traffic, select extra-durable, easily cleaned material.

Cost is a factor that varies widely, depending on whether you use old or new, expensive or relatively inexpensive fabrics. Cost may determine your choice of materials, but it need not affect the quality of your work. In this craft, it is possible to make as beautiful a rug by careful use of inexpensive materials as by purchasing new, more costly ones.

Consider ease, also. Some fabrics are obtained readily in a variety of weights, textures and colors, and some are easy to bleach or dye, and so increase the color range. Certain kinds of material can be prepared quickly for hooking and are especially easy to pull in loops through rug backing.

SUITABLE MATERIAL

Different materials will produce different effects in a hooked rug. Some fabrics, like lightweight flannel, make a flat, even surface when hooked, perfect for a rug in which texture is subordinated to design or color. Others make an uneven, nubby surface, excellent for a rug that features texture. There are materials that will create special effects, giving a light or heavy, delicate or rough appearance.

Now let us consider the use of old or new material, then specific kinds, keeping in mind the practical factors of durability, cost and ease and the aesthetic element of suitability for various effects.

USING OLD MATERIAL

Old material is usually the least expensive. It is so often used for rug-work that it has become associated with the craft. You can use material on hand, as old clothing and blankets, and supplement with a purchase of clothing from a thrift shop or community rummage sale. Friends will be glad to give you discarded clothes for your rug. *Pansy Bed,* Illustration 12, is made entirely of such clothing.

Examine old material to be sure that it is durable; you do not want fabric that is too worn. If the material looks all right, but you are uncertain of its strength, tear or cut a strip into the width you need. Then pull gently but firmly on both ends of this strip. If it breaks, the material is not durable enough and it would be a nuisance to work with, as it would undoubtedly break under the tension of

hooking. Of course, you can cut out parts of old material and discard really worn-out sections.

It takes time to prepare old material for hooking. Garments must be taken apart, hems and seams opened, buttons and zippers removed. Then the material should be washed to test for shrinkage and to make sure it is clean and colorfast. Often a vigorous washing in hot water in a washing machine will serve to tighten the weave of a fabric, making it less likely to fray or break during hooking.

It takes time also to prepare old material for special kinds of rugs. As a rule, it is hard to get a large enough quantity in the same weight. To make a rug of even texture, you will probably have to prepare different weights and combine them. To do this, cut heavy, closely-woven material into narrow strips and lightweight material into wider strips.

Careful planning is essential too with old material, as it is difficult to obtain any great amount in the same color or to match a color you want, and you must be sure to have enough of one color to complete certain areas. A problem may arise when you are using old material for background. This is usually the largest single area that must be of one color. At the end of this chapter I suggest two ways to conceal slight differences in material but it really is easier to use old material in a pattern of many small sections or in a pattern that has frequent changes in color.

Even though it takes more time to prepare old material, it can produce lovely effects. The soft, faded colors of old fabrics are excellent for reproductions of primitive rugs like *Caswell Fruit,* Color

12. PANSY BED
34-inch round

Designed by Mattie Whitney   *Hooked by the author*

An old camel's hair coat was used for the main background of this rug, a dark
brown coat for the border, an olive green skirt for the leaves, and scraps of
material from the sewing basket, yellow, pink and lavender, for the pansies.
All material was hand cut.

Plate XIII. Patterned materials, plaids, stripes, paisleys and prints, when hooked, give interesting variety to a rug. In fact, the different textures, weaves and patterns in a miscellaneous collection of old material can inspire you to make an original, artistic rug.

ADVANTAGES OF NEW FABRICS

New material has special advantages. You can make sure of durability before purchasing and can select clean, colorfast, preshrunk fabrics. You can buy just the colors you want or choose pastels that are easy to dye. You can select material easy to prepare and to hook, even buy small quantities to try out before getting the amount required to complete a rug. Finally, you can buy enough material to hook a rug in even texture or small amounts of different weights to produce variation in texture.

These advantages combine to give a single, great advantage to hookers—unlimited freedom to plan texture, color and design in a rug.

NEW MATERIAL ON A BUDGET

The single disadvantage of new material is that it is more expensive than old, but there are ways to keep cost down. Purchase material by the pound from mill-outlet stores, rather than buy it by the yard or in remnants at fabric stores. As the price of fabrics by the pound varies with different suppliers, send to several sources for samples and price lists.

Price depends on the kind of material, its weight, texture and color, and the size of pieces. Large pieces cost more than small ones. Fortunately you do not need large pieces for hooking, as you are going to cut material into narrow strips anyway. The scraps generally purchased by hookers are selvedges from blanket, coat and dress cuttings. These are long strips of woolen cloth ranging in width from about 3 to 6 inches.

Lightweight wool flannel costs more than heavier material or more open weaves. Doubtless this is because flannel has long been in demand by rugmakers for the even-textured, close-shaded rugs that are so popular. You can cut down expense by purchasing heavier materials. These will give fine effects if they are cut into narrow strips. Heavier fabrics are perfect for texture work or for bold or abstract designs.

Light-colored materials are more expensive than dark, again, probably because of demand by rugmakers who prefer light colors which are easy to dye. Usually white material is the most costly as it is used for dyeing clear light tints and is purchased in quantity by commercial suppliers of dyed material for rug-work. If you want to use light colors in a rug, you can save money by selecting pastels, as most of these can be bleached almost white, then tinted as you wish. If you like light colors slightly muted, purchase beige or pale gray to dye over; neither costs as much as white. And, of course, if you are going to use dark colors, save money by purchasing dark material. If you plan to dye it, buy a shade that is somewhat lighter than the color you want to end up with.

RUG SWATCHES

New material, especially dyed for hookers, is offered by many suppliers in a rug swatch. A swatch is a group of lightweight, wool flannel strips, usually six, each strip measuring about 3 by 8 inches. These are dyed over white material, so colors are clear, and the strips range from light to dark in closely-gradated tones. The strips are stapled at one end and are labeled with the name of the supplier and the name of the color. *Summertime*, in Color Plate XIV, is a good example of the clear, brilliant colors available in rug swatches.

Swatches come in almost unlimited colors. Here is a listing of just a few shades of green and yellow: olive-green, yellow-green, leaf-green, gold, buttercup and bronze-gold. There are many off shades, also, such as mahogany, which is six shades of brown-pink, ranging from pale blush to a deep brown-red. Talisman is a range of tones from pale yellow through peach to rosy red, and American beauty includes shades gradated from soft, medium rose to rich wine-red.

You can buy swatches in shades of gray, beige and white and even purchase swatches whose shades go together. This is how it works: Swatch I is a progression of six shades from light to medium, and Swatch II progresses, in the same color, in shades from medium to dark. Thus you have a range of twelve, carefully-gradated shades of a single color.

Manufacturers of swatches are glad to send a price list and small samples of the colors they offer. Because of the time and care taken to dye the strips, the price of a rug swatch is rather high, compared to buying an equal amount of other commercially dyed material. It would be expensive to use swatches to make a whole rug, since six strips of material measuring three by eight inches do not fill much area when hooked. However, swatches can be used in combination with home-dyed materials, keeping the swatches for small sections and filling large areas with less costly fabric.

When you want special colors and do not wish to dye material yourself, it is nice to treat yourself to a few swatches. They are ideal for small articles and especially useful as a quick, easy way to find out how closely-gradated shades work out in hooking.

ADVANTAGES OF WOOL

Whether you use old or new material, it is a good idea to know the qualities inherent in different fabrics that make them easy or difficult for rug work.

For several reasons, wool is preferred by hookers to any other material. It is readily procured either old or new and can be purchased in quantities of the same or varying weights, in different colors or in almost any amount of a single hue. Wool offers a still wider choice of color as it can be dyed easily, quickly and permanently.

Furthermore, woolen material is the most durable for a rug and is both soil resistant and easy to clean. In fact, if woolen material is washed or put through the home-dyeing process, the finished rug is washable. Finally, wool is easy to hook for it has elasticity, making it easy to pull through backing to produce loops that spread out to cover a surface quickly.

HOOKING WITH YARN

Wool rug yarn, though slightly more expensive than woolen material, is another favorite with many hookers. It is priced and sold by the skein, ball or by weight, and suppliers will send samples and price lists of the kinds they offer. Wool yarn has most of the advantages of woolen fabric, as it is readily procured in many colors, easy to dye, durable and soil resistant. Also, it makes an even surface or one of varied texture. The surface of a rug hooked with wool rug yarn has an especially soft, delicate appearance, as shown in *Textured Blocks,* Color Plate XXV, and *Moses,* Color Plate XXIV.

Although it is somewhat tedious to pull yarn through backing with a hand hook, it is possible to work rapidly with yarn by using one of the speed hooks. Since yarn can be continuously reeled, it flows without interruption through the needle eye of these tools.

Cotton rug yarn also can be hooked. It is inexpensive, available in many colors, is easy to dye and is washable. However, cotton yarn is less durable than wool and tends to absorb rather than resist dirt. Because it lacks elasticity, cotton yarn is hard to pull through backing and the loops do not spread readily to cover a surface.

There are other types of fibered materials for hooking. Sweater yarn, embroidery, needlepoint and weaving yarns can be employed to get texture variety, you can combine light- and heavyweight yarns, either as single strands or as several twisted together. Or you can combine yarn with other kinds of material to produce contrasting effects and, for greater variety, you can make loops of different heights or you can shear part of a surface.

COTTON MATERIAL

Cotton material is less expensive than either wool or yarn, and it is easy to collect cotton clothing or to buy cotton in different colors and patterns. Cotton is washable and can be dyed easily. But cotton has disadvantages for rug-work as it tends to absorb dirt and it does not wear well. Furthermore, it is hard to hook as it lacks elasticity. This means that loops do not spread but stand up stiff and straight on the surface of a rug.

Despite these disadvantages, cotton is attractive for special effects. Lightweight cottons, cut into wide strips, folded and drawn through backing, create a soft, old look. Heavy cottons, those that do not fray, like denim, sailcloth and ticking, can be cut into narrower strips and hooked to make a nubby, rough surface.

OTHER FABRICS FOR RUG-WORK

There are many other fabrics for rugs. Mixed fibered materials, cotton and rayon, wool and rayon, and elastic weaves, as jersey and crêpe, can be hooked. Tightly woven materials, felt, gabardine and serge, though somewhat difficult to pull through backing, are good for a solid, tight-looped effect. Silk and velvet are possibilities, as they are pleasant to work with and have a lovely sheen. *Flower Geometric,* Illustration 6, contains wool, jersey and cotton, and *Pansy Bed,* Illustration 12, is also of wool, jersey, and cotton.

Really, there is almost no material that cannot somehow be drawn through rug backing. So experiment with various fabrics, hooking some of each into a testing center of backing, to see the effect of each and to discover which is best for the rug you plan.

If you decide on a combination of materials for one rug, bear in mind their varying degrees of durability and the fact that some absorb dirt more quickly than others. As you will want the rug to wear and soil evenly, select equally strong, dirt-resistant fabrics for large areas and the less durable materials only for small sections.

ESTIMATING AMOUNT OF MATERIAL

You can estimate the amount of material needed for a rug by weight or by measurement.

Estimates by weight are based on the general rule that it takes about ½ pound of fabric or yarn to fill 1 square foot of backing. Of course, some workers space loops widely and use slightly less material than this, while others pack loops close and so use more. Thus, it is best to estimate a little above this standard amount to allow for individual differences and possible mistakes in dyeing. It is a great nuisance to run out of material with just a small section of rug left to finish.

To estimate by measurement, lay a single thickness of material over the surface of a pattern so as to cover it completely. Four thicknesses laid out thus will be the amount needed to fill the area. Again, I suggest you allow extra material as margin for error.

Now, if you are using different materials for background and for design, you will have to estimate two or more separate amounts. You can come close to judging correctly if you lay pieces of material, in four thicknesses, over each area. This is tedious, of course, especially if you are working with long, narrow selvedge strips. Therefore, let me assure you that with only a little experience in hooking, you will be able to judge accurately the amount of material needed to cover a given area. After hooking material into a fairly large section, it will be easy to guess how much is needed to complete areas of similar size. However, it is always wise to overestimate, to allow for mistakes and to spare yourself the trouble of having to get more material.

SPECIAL PROBLEMS

When you have estimated the amount of material needed, you will have a good idea of the cost of your rug. Sometimes, because of cost or the scarcity of a particular fabric, it is not possible to get

13. FLOWER GEOMETRIC
37 inches by 5 feet
Designed and hooked by the author

This design was adapted from a commercial pattern and the rug was made from a collection of miscellaneous materials. Several gray flannel skirts were used for the background and a man's black serge suit for the border and the scrolls and diamonds in the pattern. A wool baby blanket was used for white flowers, a jersey shirt for yellow flowers, scraps of green cotton for the leaves and pink and red cotton for the roses.

all the material at one time. Then you may find that material purchased later or from another source does not match that already hooked into the design. This can be serious, especially in background areas where it is often essential that the whole section look alike.

If you cannot get all the material you need for the background in the same color, you can conceal slight differences in these two ways: you can dye all the material for the background. Even if only a light wash of color is given, it will very likely blend the slight differences; and if the materials do not match exactly, they will still have a common cast of color and so can be used together successfully.

Another way is to divide all material for the background into four even amounts. Then mentally divide the background into four parts. Use one quarter of the material for one quarter of the background, working it in from the outside edge toward the center, with care not to end each line of hooking at the same place.

When you have used up one quarter of the material, start on the second amount in another quarter of the back-

ground. Continue working thus until all material is gone. Then, if you have to buy more material to complete the area, try to match the first as closely as possible. Divide and hook this second amount in the same way as the first, working from the uneven edge of the previous hooking toward the center of the rug. In this way, you will spread slightly different materials evenly over the rug with no sharp line of demarkation.

VARIEGATED BACKGROUND

Experienced hookers will tell you not to be too concerned about slight differences in the color of material as this seldom detracts from the appearance of a finished rug. In fact, by using two or more materials for background you can produce a beautiful, variegated effect. And you can plan this by using several kinds of material that are similar but not exactly the same color. Cut some of each, mix them, and hook them indiscriminately throughout the area for a lovely, marbleized effect or hook in swirling rows for an attractive background.

CHAPTER 6

Equipment for Making Rugs

What Tools Do I Need?

You can start hooking with a minimum of equipment. Actually, if you wish, you can begin your first rug today. I am most sympathetic with a desire to start immediately on a new hobby, and I believe also in riding the crest of one's initial enthusiasm.

To begin hooking right away, buy a rug hook and some material, and purchase either burlap or monk's cloth to serve as foundation or backing. With crayon or a felt-tipped laundry-marking pencil, draw a design on the backing. Then, with thumb tacks, mount this pattern securely on a sturdy picture frame of manageable size. Collect material with which to work from your sewing basket or clothes' closet, or buy it at a nearby thrift shop. Cut this material into narrow strips, about one-quarter inch wide, that can be drawn through the backing. You are now under way.

IMPORTANCE OF GOOD EQUIPMENT

Since my own interest in the craft and my desire to start hooking were simultaneous, I began my first rug in the fashion just described. It is the rug shown in Illustration 6. However, once happily at work, I investigated sources for tools to make the hobby easier and even more pleasant. I have found that, as in most craft work, rug-making is substantially assisted by good equipment.

So, I urge you to buy the best as soon as possible. Probably, you will find that as your family becomes interested in your work and your own enthusiasm waxes, holidays, anniversaries or birthdays will be occasions to acquire pieces of equipment. However, since everyone cannot purchase all equipment at the outset, I will list and discuss tools in what I believe is the order of importance.

41

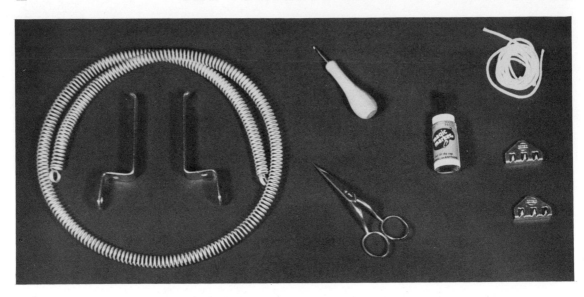

14. A HAND HOOK AND INCIDENTAL EQUIPMENT

A standard hand hook, like the one upper center, is an excellent tool to use for hooking. The other equipment is incidental but it adds ease and pleasure to rug-work. A magic marker is useful for drawing a design, bent-handled scissors are good for clipping loops, a spiral wool holder is convenient for holding cut strips, and a lacing set, shown on the right, is used to stretch backing tight, so helpful in making work easy and fast.

THE ESSENTIAL HOOK

A rug hook is the essential tool. Although it costs little, it becomes invaluable as you will come to feel that it is one of your most cherished possessions. Your hook may look exactly like another hook, but you will soon come to think it has a quality that suits you especially well.

The steel shank of my hook has a slight bend and the wooden handle a satiny finish as the result of much use. I prefer this old hook to a new one. In fact, I always keep two hooks in use alternately, as I find it annoying to break in a new one if the favorite has been misplaced. Also, by keeping an extra hook on hand, I am spared the frustration of a lost hook when I have a free moment to work.

There are several makes of rug hooks, with different-sized tips, short or long, straight, bent or with grooved handles. To be right for you, the handle of a hook should fit your hand comfortably. To work well with different weights and thicknesses of material, the tip should be large enough to grasp a variety of fabrics.

The Conventional or Standard Rug Hook, shown in Illustration 14, is a good size for most people. The handle is medium length and the tip is suited to strips of various widths.

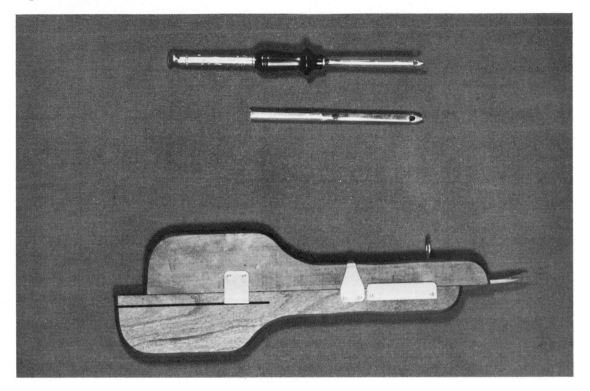

15. TWO SPEED HOOKS

Speed hooks are useful for rapid filling of large areas of background and design. They are ideal when making a rug with yarn. The tool at the top is a
Columbia Minerva DeLuxe Rug Needle. Below it is an extra needle. The speed
hook at the bottom is a Susan Burr.   Both hooks can be used with strips
of various widths and both hooks can be adjusted to make loops of different
heights.

ABOUT SPEED HOOKS

There are several kinds of special
tools for rug-work, called speed hooks.
All work on the same principle as described in the next chapter.

Illustration 15 shows two speed hooks.
The one above is a Columbia Minerva
Deluxe Rug Needle, which has two points
for use with strips of different widths.
The small needle is shown fitted into the
handle of the tool, the larger one is below
it. The metal end of the handle of this

speed hook is grooved, for adjusting to
make loops of different heights.

The speed hook at the bottom in Illustration 15 is called a Susan Burr Needle.
It, too, can be used with strips of various
widths and adjusted to make loops of
different heights.

All speed hooks are designed for fast
work, for those who want to make rugs
quickly. You many instantly put yourself
in this category. One word of caution,
however. You will not make a rug more
quickly by using this type of hook if you

do not like working with it. Many people have an unfavorable reaction to using a speed hook, as the peaceful, relaxed sensation that accompanies work with a hand hook is lost.

However, a speed hook is a time-saver, beneficial to those who want to finish a project quickly, and to those who want to make several rugs, or a very large rug, in weeks instead of months. (See Chapter 14.)

Of course, you can combine the use of a hand hook and a speed hook in the same rug. Indeed, in texture work, it is possible to get greater variety by using different tools for different sections of a pattern.

Try both a hand hook and a speed hook. At first, you will probably feel clumsy with each, but you will become proficient with a little practice. Then you can choose the tool you like best.

A FOUNDATION FOR HOOKING

Next in importance to the right hook is good material upon which to work. Obviously, you will want to insure durability of your efforts by having strong rug backing. You can use burlap, which is made of jute, or monk's cloth, which

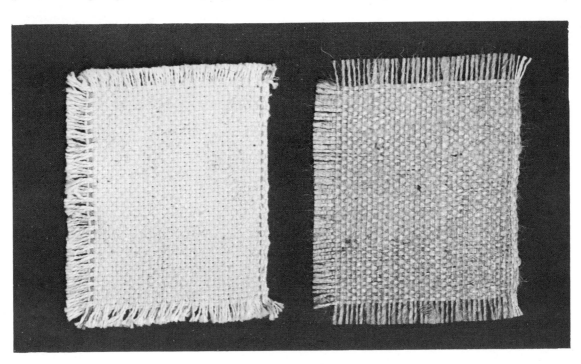

16. BURLAP AND MONK'S CLOTH

A fine grade of closely woven burlap, like that on the right of the photograph, is good for use as rug backing. Monk's cloth, shown on the left in the photograph, is a cotton fabric which is also excellent for use as backing, as it is pleasant to work on, especially durable, and needs no binding to finish edges of a rug.

is made of cotton. In Illustration 16, a small piece of burlap is shown on the right with a piece of monk's cloth on the left.

Burlap has long been popular as a base for hooked work, and most commercial patterns are printed on this fabric. If you select it, buy a good grade of closely-woven material. This is available in either a double or single weave. Double-weave burlap is fine for narrow strips, the single weave is best with wide strips that need a more open mesh if they are to be drawn through easily.

Recently I have been using a kind of monk's cloth as a foundation and I prefer this fabric to burlap. This special monk's cloth for rug-work is soft and pleasant to work on and can be used with either wide or narrow strips. The weave is uniformly even and the material can be stretched tight on a frame without fear of breaking threads. Since a cotton fabric will not crack or dry out, edges of a finished rug need only be hemmed and not bound, as with burlap, for extra protection.

Also, monk's cloth can be purchased in widths up to fifteen feet, a distinct advantage for those who plan a large rug and wish to avoid the tedious process of either sewing separate parts together or hooking through a double thickness of backing to join sections of a pattern. Monk's cloth is sold under various trade names by several suppliers and there are a number of designers who print patterns on this fabric.

STURDY FRAMES

Though many people are able to work happily without a hooking frame, I feel that easy hooking requires the steady control that a good frame gives. An ideal frame allows freedom for both hands and enables you to stretch backing tight. So, the next important piece of rug-making equipment is a sturdy frame to hold the pattern.

Frames are of two kinds, standing and lap. While both are portable, some are easier to carry than others. I will discuss standing frames first, as I consider them the easier type on which to work, especially for a beginner.

THE BLISS ADJUSTABLE RUG FRAME

There are many kinds of standing frames. I have not tried them all but I have used several different makes and I am especially pleased with the Bliss Adjustable Rug Frame, shown in Figure 12.

This frame is sometimes called the Fraser Adjustable Rug Frame, as it was designed by Harry M. Fraser. Mr. Fraser is familiar with the special requirements of a rug frame because of his wife's extensive work in hooking. As a result, the frame is well planned to suit all the needs of rug-makers.

The Bliss frame can be folded and the top section lowered, without disturbing the pattern. This makes it easy to carry or to store in a small space. The top can be lowered to a comfortable height and can be tilted to any desired angle for hooking. Also, the entire top section can be revolved, so you can inspect the underside of the work, and the top section can be removed for carrying or for placing on the floor where you can view a partly finished design at proper distance. Of great importance is the excellent hardware

FIG. 12

Figure 12. THE BLISS ADJUSTABLE RUG FRAME

This is an ideal frame for rugmaking. It permits the free use of both hands and makes it possible to stretch backing tight, an important factor in fast, easy, hooking. The frame is shown here tilted to an angle for work, with a figure in proper position. Various pieces of equipment are conveniently placed for use: a spiral wool holder, a whisk broom, and shears.

with which this frame is equipped, making it sturdy enough to hold backing tight even under the weight of a room-sized rug.

The Bliss Adjustable Rug Frame is available in five sizes: 20, 30, 40, 50, and 60 inches. These are measurements of the long crossbars to which a pattern is attached. Usually, it is best to buy a size large enough to accommodate the width of a pattern. For a beginner, it will be easier to work on a design that is attached in upright position, so the frame should be wide enough to accommodate the bottom width of the design.

No matter what size frame you buy initially, you can later purchase the two long bars and the bracing bar that make the frame longer or shorter. Generally, my hooking projects are large enough to require a 60-inch frame. But, I own a set of 40-inch bars, to shorten the frame when working on a smaller pattern that I want to carry easily to work in homes other than my own.

The Bliss Adjustable Rug Frame is made of pine, attractive as is or easy to paint or stain. Since I keep mine set up, ready for work, in a much-lived-in room, I have stained it to match the paneling there.

THE HOOP ON A STAND

The hoop on a stand, Figure 13, is another standing frame that is useful. It consists of two oval hoops, 18 by 27 inches. The top hoop is equipped with a screw at each end for fastening it to the stand. The stand, composed of two uprights with a bracing bar between, is equipped with a metal bar for tilting the hoop to a comfortable angle for hooking.

This frame is small, easy to carry and attractive. I enjoy moving mine from place to place when I want a change of scene for my work. I use it for making small hooked articles, such as mats or doorstops. I also find it a good frame for trying out small samples of design or new combinations of color. I lend the hoop on the stand to friends who want to learn to hook yet wish to make sure they like the work before investing in equipment.

Finally, when I have a rug in progress on the Bliss Adjustable Frame, I sometimes use the standing hoop for starting another pattern, one that I cannot wait to begin even though the first hooking project is not quite finished.

LAP FRAMES

Lap frames differ from standing frames in that they must be held in the lap or set on a table for work. There are several kinds, one of the best being the Puritan Portable Frame, Figure 14.

This frame is an open square of rounded metal bars set on two rounded metal legs that are braced by a wide, wooden crossbar. The bars at the top are equipped with many close-set teeth and with handles on the back and side bars. Thus, a pattern can be placed over the teeth and tightened quickly and evenly by turning the handles. It can be lifted off just as easily to shift to another section of design. Even though, at any one time, the stretched area of backing is rather small, it is possible to make a large rug on this frame.

The Puritan frame is small and light and therefore ideal for those who like to

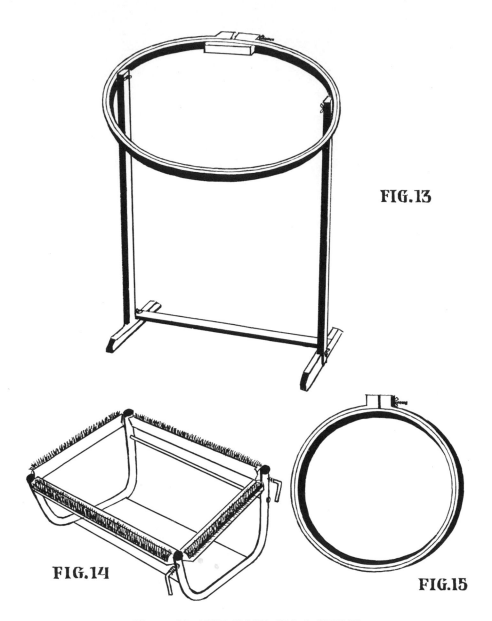

FIG.13

FIG.14

FIG.15

Figure 13. THE HOOP ON A STAND

This is a useful frame for rug work, attractive, inexpensive and easy to carry.

Figure 14. THE PURITAN PORTABLE FRAME

This sturdy lap frame is perfect for those who have limited space, for those who want portable equipment and for the curl-up-in-a-chair hooker. It is possible to make a large rug on this frame.

Figure 15. THE LAP HOOP

This is one of the least expensive frames and is especially useful as a piece of extra equipment on which to make small hooked articles, such as mats or doorstops, or as a place to try out designs and combinations of color.

carry their work with them. It is perfect, too, for the curl-up-in-a-chair hooker and those who are confined to bed and want to do handwork.

The Lap Hoop, Figure 15, is one of the least expensive frames available for rug-hooking. It is a 14-inch round and, like the hoop on a stand, is equipped with a screw on the top section for tightening this band onto the lower one.

It is easy to place backing on a lap hoop and equally easy to remove it from this frame. However, it is somewhat difficult to work on the lap hoop, to keep both hands free for hooking, since the hoop must be held with one hand. If the hoop is just laid on the lap, it tends to wobble as a loop is pulled through the backing. This is especially true since a beginner, who is just learning to pull loops through, tends to tug more vigorously than an experienced hooker.

To solve the problem, I place one side of the hoop against my waist and brace the other side against the arm of a chair. Thus wedged in, I am able to work fairly easily and rapidly on this frame.

At the start, you can learn to hook on a lap hoop rather than invest in more expensive equipment. Eventually, as it makes work easier and quicker, you will probably want to buy a better frame. If so, you can still use the lap hoop as a piece of secondary equipment in ways suggested for the hoop on a stand. Or use it, as I do, when traveling, for it is the only frame I know that will fit into a suitcase.

A picture frame or a canvas stretcher can also be used for hooking. Like the lap hoop, either is hard to hold steady while working but can serve as inexpensive equipment with which to begin.

MECHANICAL STRIPPERS FOR RUG-WORK

Many hookers cut material by hand for rug-work. Rugs made this way can be just as durable and beautiful as those for which a mechanical cutter was used. However, mechanical strippers cut material so quickly and evenly that they are a real boon to rugmakers and once you have seen how they work, you will certainly want to own one. Though relatively expensive, they are fine precision tools that should last a lifetime.

There are several makes of mechanical strippers and different models of each make. Some models can be set on any surface, others are equipped with a screw for clamping onto a table top. All have a handle for turning the steel blade that cuts material into strips, and most models can be fitted with various blade sizes, for cutting either narrow or wide strips. For example, the Bliss strip slitter has three models: Model A cuts strips of a width for hooked rugs only, Model B for both braided and hooked rugs, and Model E cuts for both braided and hooked rugs and is equipped with a power unit for electric operation.

I use a table Bliss Strip Slitter, Model A, the one shown in Illustration 17. I prefer this to a clamp-on model as I sometimes use my cutter away from home and do not want to risk marring someone else's table.

There are blade sizes to fit Model A, numbered 3, 4, 5, 6 and 8. Number 3 blade cuts six strips of material at one

17. A MECHANICAL CUTTER

There are several makes of mechanical cutters for rug-work. Like the Bliss Strip Slitter shown here, they can be used to cut material quickly and evenly and can be fitted with blades of different sizes for cutting wide or narrow strips. A number 3 blade is being used here, to cut six strips at once, each strip $\frac{3}{32}$ inches wide.

time, each $\frac{3}{32}$ of an inch wide; Number 4 cuts five strips, $\frac{1}{8}$ inch wide; Number 5, four strips, $\frac{5}{32}$ of an inch wide; Number 6, three strips, $\frac{3}{16}$ of an inch wide, and Number 8, two strips, $\frac{1}{4}$ inch wide.

One blade, the size you request, is included in the price of a stripper. If you do not specify size, your tool will be equipped with a Number 4 blade. This is a good size with which to begin as it cuts medium-wide strips that can be used either for rather fine detail or for

rapid filling of larger areas. Eventually, you may want to use other sizes which you can order at any time. Also, if a blade becomes dull through much use, you can return it and receive a new blade for a minimal charge.

I like a Number 3 blade for shaded work, where many strips are hooked into a small area of design, such as flowers, stems and leaves. In this type of rug, I use a Number 4 to cut material for background, as wider strips fill an area more quickly. When hooking a bold or primitive pattern, I prefer a Number 6 blade, partly because it increases the speed in filling and partly because loops of wide strips give a rough, nubby texture to the surface of a pattern.

I often work with several different blade sizes for a single rug in order to use material of different weights and still retain even texture. For instance, when hooked, heavy wool cut on a Number 3 will blend with lightweight material cut on a Number 6 blade.

All strippers come with complete instructions on use and care. Rugmakers frequently buy one jointly, a practical plan, since with this tool it is easy to cut enough material in an hour to last for several days of hooking. However, I have noted that an ardent hooker usually wants full ownership of a stripper as soon as possible. After you have used a mechanical cutter, it is annoying to cut material by hand when you run out of strips and the shared tool is not readily available.

INCIDENTAL EQUIPMENT FOR ADDED PLEASURE

There is much incidental equipment that adds ease and pleasure to rugwork. Buy basic tools first and, when you can, purchase these nice extras.

Scissors with bent handles are made especially for rug-hooking. The bent handle makes it easy to cut drawn up ends on the surface of a design, and a small groove in the tip of these scissors makes possible the rapid insertion of the blade into a loop to cut through it.

There are several makes and sizes of bent-handled scissors. I like a small pair, like that shown in Illustration 14, because

it is light and easy to handle. I buy the best I can afford and keep them just for hooking. For convenience, I hang my scissors on a drapery hook inserted into the backing, as shown in Figure 12. While you will enjoy using a pair of these special scissors, you can use any small pair of sharp scissors for clipping loops and ends of strips. Of course, for shearing a whole rug, or a large portion of one, you will need a pair of large, heavy scissors.

The Magic Marker, also shown in Illustration 14, is an excellent tool for drawing a design. It is available in different colors, has a slanted felt tip for drawing either a broad or fine line and is so easy to work with that it almost seems to inspire a free, flowing movement of the hand. Also, with this indelible pencil, you can darken any faint lines in a commercial pattern, mark a date and initials on a pattern, if you wish, or re-draw sections of a commercial design. Incidentally, a Magic Marker is useful, too, for marking articles of clothing, such as boots and raincoats that will not take a sew-on tape.

For binding edges of a finished rug, use cotton rug tape, the sew-on, not the iron-on kind. This is available in several different colors and if you cannot find a color to match the background of your rug, you can buy a light shade that can easily be dyed to match.

For sewing on binding or for hemming a rug, you will need a spool of strong carpet thread. To clean lint and clipped ends off the surface of a pattern, you should have a small, stiff brush. A whisk broom or vegetable brush is satisfactory to brush the hooked area, for neatness and to show clearly how your work is progressing.

For use on a standing frame such as

the Bliss, there are two essentials and two extras. You will need carpet tacks for mounting backing on the bars. One-half inch is a good size, long enough to stay in under the pressure of hooking and not so large that they split the wood of the bar. A lacing set is necessary, also, to secure the backing to the side bars. There are several kinds of commercial lacing sets, one of which, the Dritz Rug Lacing Set, is shown in Illustration 14. This set consists of sixteen hooks and a length of cord. Eight hooks are placed on side arms of the frame, four to a side. The remaining hooks are inserted into the backing, four on each side, and the cord is used to lace back and forth between these hooks. If you do not want to buy a lacing set, you can use drapery hooks and heavy string to make a home-lacing arrangement.

The Spiral Wool Holder is a delightful extra. Shown in Illustration 14, it also is intended for use with a standing frame like the Bliss. It comes in different sizes to fit a long or short frame. The holder consists of a spring that stretches across the top bar and is fastened at each end to metal uprights shown in the picture. The strips of cut material are then strung along the length of the spring thus providing easy selection of whatever color is desired. Also, as a clothesline of colored strips, the wool holder adds to the attractiveness of a hobby center.

The final piece of equipment designed for use on a standing frame is a Rug Lamp. There are several makes, each with fittings to attach to the side arm of the frame. They are goose-necked, so light can be directed on any portion of the work, and shaded so that the light is not reflected into the eyes of the worker.

While this special lamp is convenient and helpful for hooking, any light that brightens the work area and does not reflect is satisfactory. You can make a good lighting arrangement at home by fastening a wall lamp above your frame or by placing a standing lamp beside it. Be sure to use a daylight bulb, for fluorescent light tends to change the appearance of colors.

A WIDE CHOICE OF EQUIPMENT

Today's wide choice of equipment is the result of an increased demand for good tools for rug-work. You may well feel overwhelmed by the range and wish to buy just the necessary tools with which to begin. Hookers have worked for years with no extras to aid them, and you can certainly enjoy the craft today with only basic equipment. However, it is pleasant to know that you can readily increase the ease and pleasure of your hobby by purchasing, whenever you wish, the various fine tools now available.

NECESSARY EQUIPMENT

1. Hand Hook or Speed Hook
2. Burlap or Special Monk's-Cloth Backing
3. Standing or Lap Frame
4. Scissors
5. Whisk Broom
6. Carpet Thread and Needle

NICE TO HAVE

1. Mechanical Stripper
2. Indelible Marking Pencil
3. Rug-lacing Set
4. Spiral Wool-Holder
5. Rug Lamp

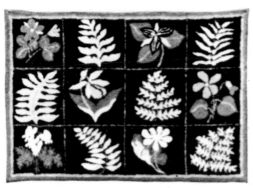

I. WOODLAND
30 by 40 inches
Black provides a dramatic background for the
pastel design colors.

II. GABRIEL
18 by 40 inches
The elongated figure makes this a handsome
hearthside rug or hanging.

III. OWL EYES
18 by 36 inches
Muted design colors are set off by the bright-
color background.

IV. FAMILY TREE
30 by 40 inches
Shaded leaves act as foil for brilliant-color fruit.

V. SEASCAPE
28 by 40 inches
Flowing design lines and delicate colors suit
this theme.

VI. FLOWER FANCY
30 by 40 inches
Yarn leftovers were used for the multi-hued
abstract flowers.

Designed by Heidi Gilmartin for Heritage Hill Patterns.
Hooked by the author, using punch needle and yarn.

VII. NOAH'S ARK
30 by 45 inches
Bright, flat colors are suited to this design.

VIII. LION AND LAMB
27 by 40 inches
A design adapted from Edward Hick's painting—"The Peaceable Kingdom"

IX. SPRINGTIME
30 by 42 inches
Simplified shading gives the flowers a clean, crisp look.

X. RING AROUND THE ROSY
36 by 54 inches
Bright, flat colors in an all-direction design.

XI. SUNBURST
27 by 44 inches
Angular rays and leaves provide contrast to center circle.

XII. HEARTS AND FLOWERS
36 by 54 inches
Pastel colors are appropriate to this old-valentine motif.

Designed by Dolli Tingle for Heritage Hill Patterns.
Shown painted on cardboard, a step in planning a rug design.

XIII. CASWELL FRUIT
26 by 66 inches
Edana Design
Hooked by Alice Beatty
Adapted from section of an antique rug—
Caswell Carpet, made in 1835.

XIV. SUMMERTIME
30 by 45 inches
Designed by Dolli Tingle
Hooked by the author
Realism with simplified shading, and black
background for drama.

XV. IN THE MEADOW
Heirloom Pattern
Hooked by Connie Charleson
A masterpiece of realistic shading.

XVI. THE MORGAN
24 by 36 inches
Designed by Mona Van Vliet
Hooked by Mary Jarry
Old whaling ship reproduced in beautifully
simple design.

XVII. SQUARE RIGGER
30 by 34 inches
Designed by Dolli Tingle
Hooked by Hans Vierling
An unusual color choice for a nautical motif.

XVIII. SIGNATURE
18 by 36 inches
Designed and hooked by Heidi Gilmartin
Husband's initials in international flag code.

CHAPTER 7

Techniques of Hooking

How Shall I Start Hooking?

You are now ready with a frame and a hook of your choice and have purchased a design, or you have drawn one of your own on backing. There is but one more step of preparation.

STITCHING THE EDGES

Before placing the backing on a frame, make a single ½-inch fold along the raw edges of the material. Either hand-stitch or machine-stitch this down to keep the edges from raveling.

This ½-inch fold prepares the backing for use on any frame except the hoops, the standing oval, or round lap type. There is a special problem with these because rug backing generally extends only a few inches beyond the edges of a design. This is not enough material to fasten between hoops when you are working on outside areas of a pattern.

To solve the problem, prepare the backing for use on hoops by making a single ½-inch fold on all the outside edges and either hand-stitch or machine-stitch this down. Then sew a 6- to 8-inch strip of extra material onto this fold. You can use sheeting or large scraps from your sewing box.

This bordering material increases the size of the backing so that it can be fastened securely between the hoop sections when you work on corners and outside edges. You can remove the extra material when you are through hooking and are ready to hem or bind the finished rug.

FASTENING MATERIAL "AS TIGHT AS POSSIBLE"

It is important to stretch backing tight on a frame. If you are using a picture frame or canvas stretcher, fasten the backing with thumbtacks or ½-inch carpet tacks, spacing them about 2 inches apart. Thumbtacks are easy to remove when you shift a pattern to another area for work, but they sometimes pop out under the pressure of hooking. Carpet tacks are harder to remove but will not come out of a frame during work.

Center the area of design that you plan to work on first within the circumference of the frame and stretch the backing as tightly and as evenly as possible when you tack it on the frame.

If you are using a hoop, lay the backing over the lower section of the hoop; then place the top section over this. Tighten the top section onto the lower section by turning the screw that draws the top section together. With material held between the hoops, pull gently but firmly on all edges, thus easing out wrinkles on the surface and drawing the material tight.

If you use the Puritan Lap Frame, lay the backing on top of the toothed bars and pull it along the outside edges to secure it on the teeth. Then, reach under the material and turn outward the two bars that are equipped with handles, thus drawing the backing tight.

To put backing on the Bliss Adjustable Rug Frame, or one similar to it, tack the bottom edge of the pattern onto the lower bar, spacing the tacks about 2 inches apart. Then, tack the top edge to the upper bar. Tighten the screws at each end of the lower bar. Now, loosen the screws that secure the upper bar and turn this bar outward to roll excess backing until it is drawn as tight as possible. Finally, tighten the screws that keep this bar from slipping.

Next, lace the side edges of the backing to the nearest side bars of the frame. Pull firmly and evenly as you lace, to make the hooking surface still more taut. Now loosen the screws that hold the top section of the frame in position. Lower this section to the proper height for you, and tilt it to a comfortable angle for hooking.

I cannot stress too much the importance of having backing stretched tight. Time taken to retighten it as it loosens under the pressure of hooking is time well spent. Your hooking will be more even, faster and more enjoyable if the material upon which you are working is absolutely taut.

YOUR WORK AREA

Now you are ready to select a pleasant, well-lighted place to work. Choose a comfortable, straight-backed chair and sit close to the work so you will not have to lean forward or down. Then *relax*.

Figure 12 shows a Bliss Adjustable Rug Frame with backing tacked on, laced and rolled. The frame is tilted to an angle for hooking, with a figure in proper position to work. Various pieces of equipment are conveniently placed for use: a spiral wool-holder, a whisk broom and rug-hooking scissors.

FILLING AND PACKING

Hooking is the process of pulling strips of material through openings in the weave of a foundation fabric, with strips pulled from the back of the fabric to the front and placed as a series of loops.

Setting a number of loops into backing is called "filling."

Close filling of one fabric with loops of another material is called "packing" and packing suggests just what it accomplishes. By pulling enough loops through the backing, you will increase tension in the mesh of this fabric, and increased tension will serve to enclose loops so tight that they cannot slip out. You can remove single rows of loops easily, by pulling one end of a strip, but it is quite difficult to remove a strip from a packed area.

It is perfectly all right to pull out strips that you have used for practice and use them again in a rug, and you can realign slightly enlarged holes in the mesh of a practice area by rubbing your fingertips briskly over this section.

HANDLING THE HOOK

Select an area of background on a pattern on which to practice and begin work with a hand hook. (The use of speed hooks will be discussed later.) There are two ways to grip a hand hook. You can pick it up as you would a pencil, and many people work rapidly and evenly holding the hook this way. Or you can use the whole-hand grip. Either is correct, so use the one that is easier for you.

I prefer the whole-hand grip as I feel it gives me more wrist control to make loops of an even height. Also, I find it less tiring when I am hooking for long periods or working with heavy material.

For the whole-hand grip, grasp the wooden handle of the hook firmly in the palm of your right hand. Place your index finger on the steel shank, about halfway between the curved tip of the hook and

the place where the shank is set into the handle, as shown in Figure 16.

With your left hand, pick up a strip of material, cut to a width for hooking. Hold the strip about one inch from the end, between the thumb and index finger, as in Figure 17.

To be in position to hook, put your left hand under the backing and up against it at the point where you plan to start. Place your right hand on top of the backing with the tip of the hook just slightly to the right of your left hand.

HOOKING IN A STRAIGHT LINE

Start practice work by hooking in a straight line. Work from right to left, making a row of loops that follow a horizontal thread in the backing.

First, insert the curved tip of the hook through an opening in the mesh, with the curve facing in the direction you are going. With your left hand, lay the end of the strip across the tip of the hook and then draw this end up through the backing. Continue holding on to the strip with your left hand, allowing the part that is being drawn up to glide between thumb and index finger.

You now have a short length of strip standing up in the backing on the surface of the rug and are prepared to make the first loop. Using the horizontal thread of the backing as a guide for a straight row, skip one hole in the mesh and insert the hook in the next opening. Lay the strip across the tip of the hook and gently ease a section of it up into a loop on the surface of the backing, as shown in Figure 18.

Continue, in this way, to make a row

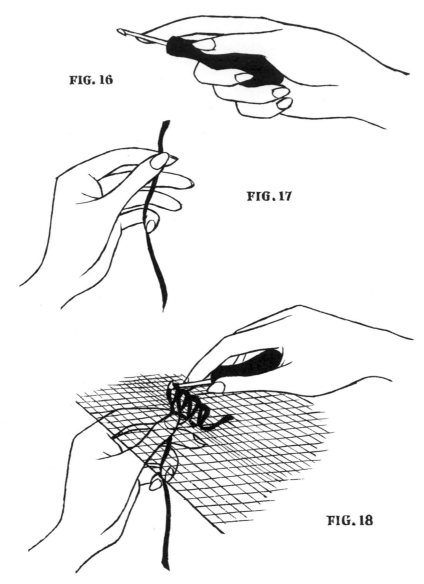

FIG. 16

FIG. 17

FIG. 18

Figure 16. HOLDING THE HOOK

This is the whole-hand grip, a good way to hold a rug hook as it gives wrist control for making loops of even height.

Figure 17. HOLDING A STRIP OF MATERIAL

A strip of material cut to a width for hooking is held in the left hand in this fashion.

Figure 18. MAKING A ROW OF LOOPS

A section of the cut strip is brought up through an opening in the mesh of the backing into a loop on the surface. Here the loops are set in a line following the horizontal thread of the backing.

of closely-set loops. When you come to the end of the first strip, draw this end through to the top of the backing. Then, after you have filled a small area, you can clip all the ends to the same height as the loops.

HOOKING THE SECOND STRIP

Now start with a second strip. Bring the end up in the same opening as the final end of the first strip, then continue hooking until you have made a long line of loops.

Try making a second row just above the first. Make this row two threads above the lower one and your work will look like the two straight lines of loops in Illustration 18.

You have begun to pack when you have completed two rows of loops close together. Continue packing by making several more rows, one just above the other. You will notice that each successive

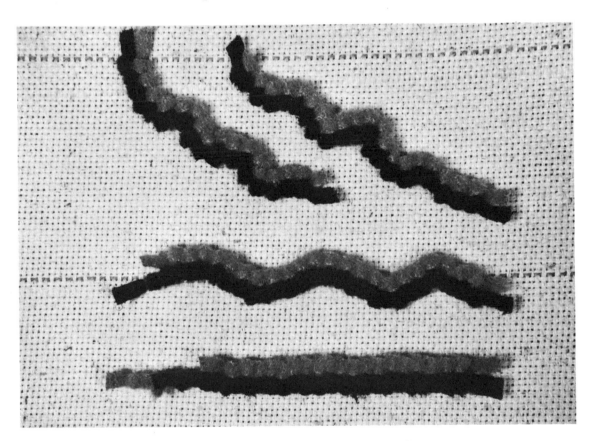

18. PRACTICE ROWS OF HOOKING

In these rows of practice hooking, the double row at the bottom is hooked from right to left, following a horizontal thread of the backing. The rows just above are hooked horizontally from right to left in a wavy line. The two rows of hooking in the upper part of the photograph are done from right to left, a wavy line angled in a vertical direction.

row is easier to hook as packing has opened up the holes in the mesh surrounding the packed section.

A WORKING RHYTHM

Sometimes it is helpful to think of the hooking technique as a series of separate movements: (1) insertion of hook in backing; (2) laying over of a strip by the left hand; (3) slight downward pressure of right forefinger on the hook to open up the mesh and allow the loop to be drawn through easily; (4) a slight downward and outward movement of the right wrist to release the tip of the hook from a drawn-up loop.

If you accidentally pull out the previous loop each time you draw up the next loop, it is probably because you are holding the strip too tight with your left hand. Try to have the feeling that you are handing the loop to the hook with your left hand, then release your grip on the strip enough to allow your right hand to raise the loop to the surface of the backing. If you will lay one loop carefully against the preceding one and slightly exaggerate the wrist movement to release the tip of hook from the loop, you will soon sense a rhythm in hooking. A steady, regular rhythm is your first goal, with no concern for speed.

Soon your first awkwardness will pass and, as your hands learn what to expect of one another, all these seemingly separate movements will synchronize into an easy, flowing motion.

HOOKING IN A WAVY LINE

When you have gained confidence hooking in a straight line, try hooking in a wavy line. Working from right to left across the backing, make a curving row of loops. Then make a second row of loops just above this, following the curves of the first row. The center section of Illustration 18 shows two wavy rows of loops, going horizontally across the backing, with the top row directly above the lower one and following its curves.

Now practice making wavy rows in a vertical direction, angled slightly from right to left. Start at bottom of the backing and work toward the top. Hook two rows next to each other, like those in the upper part of Illustration 18.

Next, hook a wavy line starting at the top of the backing and working toward the bottom. Keep loops close together. Do not try to count the threads of the backing because you must start to judge how close to set your loops.

HOW MUCH TO PACK

Your purpose is to make a rug surface that will be both durable and beautiful. If you overpack, by pulling too much material up through the backing, you will stretch and weaken the foundation fabric. Furthermore, a rug that is overpacked tends to "hump up" on the floor. But if you underpack, by not putting in enough material, the backing may show through, the surface will look uneven and your rug will not be as durable.

The width of strips and weight of material that you use determine the number of holes that you need to fill for proper packing. Naturally, you will need to put in fewer loops of wide strips than of narrow ones, and if you are using heavy material, you will need fewer loops than of a lighter weight material.

The type of material also makes a difference in the number of holes to fill. Some materials, those with elasticity, such as wool, have a lot of "spread" and therefore a drawn-up loop covers more surface than just the area over the hole through which it has been drawn. Cotton and other materials that are tight and stiff do not spread. So, when using this kind of material, you will have to make more loops in order fully to cover a surface.

You will soon learn to judge packing by feel as well as by appearance. The satisfaction of putting in the last few necessary loops to provide a snug fit is quite different from the struggle to tug in more loops than the backing can comfortably hold.

AVOID AWKWARD DIRECTION, "CROSS-OVERS" AND LOOSE ENDS

It is easy to hook straight rows from right to left or to make angled rows in this direction. But, it is difficult to hook from left to right and work becomes slow and uneven as soon as the direction of hooking becomes awkward.

You may try to hook in an awkward direction in order to save time by not having to cut a strip. In rug work, however, no time is saved by hooking each strip to the end, and it is all right to use a short strip, one that may only be long enough to make two or three loops. So when direction becomes awkward cut off the strip and draw the end to the top of the backing. Then start again in an easy direction with the remaining piece of the strip.

Always bring each loop up close to the preceding loop. Many hookers are tempted to draw a strip along under the backing and pull up a few loops at a short distance from where they are filling. The temptation occurs when you work with a color and decide to insert some of the same color in a nearby area.

Short lengths of strips drawn across the back of a rug to avoid taking time to cut and start again, are called "cross-overs." Since these lie slightly above the rest of a hooked area on the back of a rug, as shown in the lower area of Illustration 19, they receive the first friction of use and so wear out quickly.

When you begin to hook rapidly, you may inadvertently make cross-overs. A quick way to find out whether you have done so is to run your fingers across the back of a rug on a finished area. You will feel cross-overs if they are there and you may also find end pieces that have not been drawn up. Clip all cross-overs and draw the two ends to the top of the backing. Draw up any other dangling ends also. By doing this you will make a neater, more durable rug.

HEIGHT OF LOOPS

For most rugs, it is important to have all loops the same height. However, hookers differ as to the best height. A general rule of ⅛- to ¼-inch is good. For fine, needlepoint texture, a ⅛-inch loop is best. For heavier texture, pull the loops higher, and for special effects, pull loops to any height you like.

I raise loops to about ¼ inch, unless I want particular textural effects. Since a certain amount of surface material makes

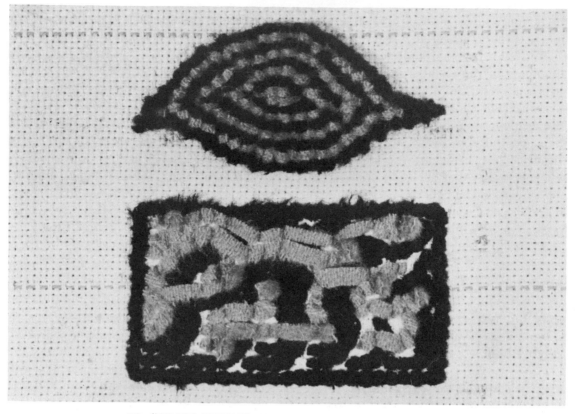

19. "CROSS-OVERS" AND DIRECTIONAL HOOKING

The small area of hooking in the lower part of the photograph is shown from the reverse side. It reveals a number of cross-overs, short lengths of strips drawn along under the surface of the work. Avoid making cross-overs for these bits of fabric will wear out quickly, as they lie slightly above the rest of the hooked surface and so receive the first friction of use.

The simplified leaf design in the upper part of the photograph is an example of directional hooking, showing how filling rows of hooking follow the curve of the outline rows of a design.

a rug wear longer, I feel that shorter loops are rather impractical. I raise loops higher if I plan to cut loops or shear part of the rug for texture variety, since, by shearing, I will remove some of the wearing surface.

You will soon find a loop height that is right for your purpose, one that is both practical and attractive. Also, you will discover that your wrist movement, in releasing each loop at the same height, soon

becomes automatic. In fact, if you decide to do an area of higher or lower loops for a special effect, you will have to adjust to this change as your wrist will have become set in an accustomed way.

Your first loops may be quite uneven but, with practice, you will learn to hook rapidly, making loops of exactly the same height. Please do not spoil your pleasure in rug-work by being too critical. Just remember the main goal in this craft is imaginative, individual work. Do not become discouraged by scrutinizing loops too carefully at the eye-level of your frame for eventually the rug will be seen from a greater distance. Slight variations in height can be pressed out with a steam iron when you have finished a pattern, or they will soon be "walked out" when the rug is in use. Furthermore, a slight unevenness can give a rug a desirable, handmade look.

HOW SPEED HOOKS WORK

Speed hooks are a form of shuttle, with material threaded through a needle eye in the point of the tool. These tools, instead of lifting loops to the surface of the backing, as with a hand hook, are used to push loops through the mesh from the front to the back. For this, backing must be stretched especially tight, as the pushing technique requires a resistant surface.

Some speed hooks can be used with both strips of fabric and with yarn, others can be used only with yarn. All speed hooks are really better suited to yarn since this can be continuously reeled, thus avoiding the tedious rethreading of the tool that is necessary with short fabric strips. Complete directions for use of the Columbia-Minerva DeLuxe Punch Needle are given in Chapter 14.

DIRECTIONAL HOOKING

You have practiced hooking in a straight line, going from right to left, following a horizontal thread in the backing.

You have found that you can hook just as easily in a slanting, wavy line, either vertically or horizontally. If you have filled an area of any size with these two different directions, you may have noticed that each gives a quite different effect.

You can plan an effect by hooking continuously in a particular direction. This is called "directional hooking" and it can be used to good advantage, as to accent a curve. For example, when hooking a leaf, you can produce a soft, curving effect by making rows of hooking follow the curve of the outside edge of the leaf. Filling lines will then be a series of rows following the curve of the outline row. The simple leaf design in Illustration 19, shows directional hooking, with rows all following the curve of the outside edge.

You can use the same technique to accent angles. I have used directional hooking to play up rays of a large sunburst motif in the center of a room-sized rug. First, I outlined the rays and hooked filling rows in the same direction. Then, I worked the entire background of the rug in straight rows, running crosswise against the direction of the rays. This rug, *The Beehive*, is shown in Illustration 20.

To achieve variety in a rug, you can use areas of straight-line hooking that contrast with areas of curved lines. The two lower samples of hooking in Illustration 21 show the contrasting effect of these two directions.

To make the background of a rug unobtrusive, do not hook continually in any one direction. Instead, work the entire area in short, curving lines. These are called "rivers." First, hook several rivers through an area, then join them with rows

20. THE BEEHIVE
9 by 15 feet

Designed by George Wells　　　　　　　　　　　　*Hooked by the author*

In this dramatic design, the rows of hooking follow the direction of the design. The rows in the sunburst follow the direction of the rays and the rows in the background are hooked horizontally, going against the direction of the rays and thus helping to accent the design.

In order to make the rug in one piece, I tacked finishing nails at 2-inch intervals along all four bars of a 60-inch Bliss Rug Frame. Then I stretched the backing over these, just as one would place a curtain on a curtain stretcher, and worked one section of the rug at a time. (Photograph by Bill Margerin. Courtesy *Living for Young Homemakers.*)

21. EFFECTS OF DIRECTIONAL HOOKING

Directional hooking is used to gain special effects. An area of straight lines gives a different effect from an area worked in wavy rows, as shown by the two small areas of hooking in the lower part of the photograph. A background whose rows do not follow any single direction continually, as illustrated in the upper section of the photograph, can be made to look flat and solid as a foil for directional hooking of a design.

that go in a different direction. The dark rows in the upper part of Illustration 21 are short rivers, the light lines are the joining rows. After working a number of rivers and joining them, you can fill the little "lakes" that are left.

A background hooked in rivers will look flat and solid and be an excellent foil for emphasis on design. You can use the same method to emphasize background, by working with materials that are mottled or of slightly different shades. Such material, when hooked in short curving rows, gives a subtle variety to a background.

"PAINTING WITH WOOL" FOR REALISTIC EFFECTS

The technique of hooking realistic designs in natural colors is sometimes called "painting with wool," and it achieves an astonishingly close duplication of nature. It is a favorite technique with many hookers, requiring some skill and employing fine wool material, cut into very narrow strips and dyed in many, closely-related shades of color.

In this realistic work, hookers often use six or more shades of a single color, ranging from a tint to a deep "shadow" hue in one small flower. Strips must be narrow, of course, to fit many shades into so small an area of design, and shades must be closely gradated so they will blend for a painted effect.

The basic principle in painting with wool is the same as that in realistic painting. To achieve depth, the darkest areas of color are those farthest from the eye of a viewer, the light section is closest and medium shades fill in between. For example: in an apple, the lightest shade of red might be at the center, the front of the apple, the color graduating from this through several deeper shades to the darkest crimson at the outer edge of the fruit. This shading gives an effect of roundness. In hooking a flower, depth and contour are gained by using the darkest color at the base or throat, the lightest shade on the forward edges of the petals, with several medium shades between to make a close blend.

Painting with wool, or shading as it is usually called, is not really difficult once you understand the principle involved. Besides, there is a wealth of information to help you with this technique. You can buy diagrams of flowers, fruits, leaves, scrolls and many other designs. You can purchase these as single sheets of instruction on a particular design, or as books and pamphlets devoted entirely to diagrams for use in making realistic rugs. You can paint with wool by using a dia-gram or, if you are a natural artist, as many people are without realizing it, you can make a realistic rug by emulating shadings of color in nature.

Diagrams for realistic hooking are similar to numbered, fill-in paintings sold in art and hobby stores. They are easy to follow if you have the required number of proper shades on hand. Diagrams are numbered, lettered or accompanied by a key of symbols, with these indicating the shade to be hooked into a given area of the design. Usually, the lightest shade is given the first number or letter. For example: Number 1 indicates the lightest shade, Number 2, the next darkest shade and so on. In addition to instruction on where to place shades, many diagrams even give suggestion on what colors to use.

Figure 19 is an example of a diagram for hooking a flower, using six shades of one color.

"SAW-TOOTHING" AND "FINGERING"

There are two hooking tricks to blend shades more closely. One is called "saw-toothing," the other "fingering."

Saw-toothing is the process of hooking single loops just to one side of the row that is being worked, so as to make little points into an unhooked area, as with the teeth of a saw. After doing this, hook in the shade of the adjoining section to fill gaps between these "teeth." The lower right area of hooking in Illustration 22 shows saw-toothing. Here, single loops from the main area of light color were hooked into an unfilled section, then loops of a dark color were hooked between.

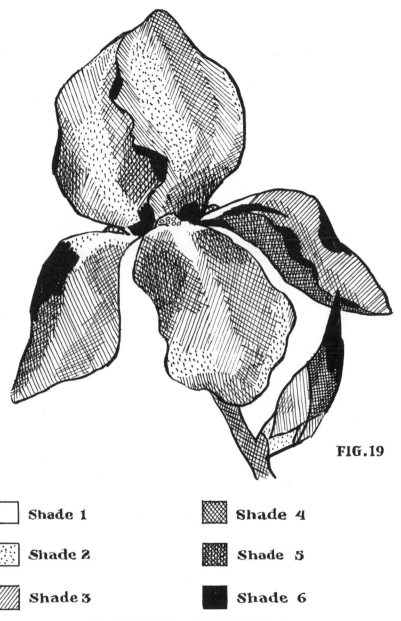

FIG.19

☐ Shade 1		▨ Shade 4	
▨ Shade 2		▨ Shade 5	
▨ Shade 3		■ Shade 6	

Figure 19. A DIAGRAM FOR SHADING AN IRIS

Closely graded shades of color, from light to dark, are used for a realistic effect.
This is sometimes called "painting with wool."

Fingering is the process of hooking a series of single, low rows into an area that is to be filled. These rows, used often in flower petals and leaves, give an effect of delicate veining. Sometimes, to make them look especially fine and narrow, fingering rows are clipped across the top. The upper right area of hooking in Illustration 22 shows a petal with a few fingering rows.

22. SAW-TOOTHING, FINGERING AND HIGH-LIGHTING

These are special techniques of hooking, used to gain a certain effect. Saw-toothing, shown in the lower right corner of the photograph, helps to increase the blending of shades. Fingering, shown in the petal design in the upper right section of the photograph, gives an effect of delicate veining. High-lighting is a means of gaining an effect of realism with only a few shades of color. It is shown, slightly exaggerated, in the pear.

THE FUN OF SHADING

It is fun to paint with wool, to master fine shading and make realistic hooked rugs. This particular technique is often associated with the craft, and many commercial designs have been planned as inspiration and challenge to the hooker who wants to do intricate scrolls, tiny buds and blossoms and turning leaves.

However, I have found that fine-shaded rugs sometimes blurr through use to an unfortunate degree. Practically speaking, I think extremely close shading is better for hooked pictures, pillow tops or chair seats than for rugs. Furthermore, I think you can achieve a realistic effect and retain differences in shades permanently by a much simpler technique.

"HIGH-LIGHTING" FOR REALISM

By "high-lighting," it is possible to get a realistic effect that will last through years of use on the floor. With this technique, only a few shades are used, and these are meant to blend but not melt into one another. You are really working with color blocks and the eye does the mixing. Again, the principle is the same as that used in painting.

To high-light, hook a patch of your lightest shade on the forward surface of a design. Next hook a medium shade to fill middle sections, and finally hook the darkest color for the area farthest from the viewer. With just three shades, you can get an effect of depth and contour.

Illustration 22 shows high-lighting in a pear, slightly exaggerated to give you the idea. As the fruit is tilted, the light area appears on the forward surface at lower left, the medium shade fills most of the remaining area, except for the shadow section done in the darkest hue on the right (back) edge.

DRAMATIC EFFECTS THROUGH COLOR, LINE AND TEXTURE

Of course, there are no rules that you require to shade at all, whether realistically or as high-lighting. Actually, satisfying effects in rugs, as in other decorative media, are often the result of a complete departure from realism.

You may observe this in your home where the trees on your white draperies may be blue or the stems, leaves and flowers on your green wallpaper may be gold. But, the total effect is good, and total effect is the main consideration in rugmaking.

Color, line and texture, in themselves, can be dramatic. Texture can be varied by contrasting heights of loops, opposing cut and uncut loops or by using materials of differing widths and weights. The soft spread of wool will contrast sharply with the tight-looped appearance of cotton. Yarn in combination with other materials will add interesting variety to the surface of a rug.

In fact, there is an almost endless number of techniques and materials to give beauty to a hooked pattern. You might like to experiment by making a gay, striped rug that will offer a fine chance to try out different techniques and fabrics. You can make an inexpensive rug this way. In brief, give free rein to your imagination, learn much and have a lot of fun.

HOOKING YOUR FIRST RUG

When you have practiced hooking, know which tool you prefer and have considered the total effect you want, you are ready to start your first hooked rug. Perhaps you wonder just where to start.

If you are using the Bliss Adjustable Rug Frame, or something similar with backing tacked on, laced and rolled, it is sensible to start at the bottom of the pattern and fill in the area as far as you can comfortably reach. Then, roll this area under and work on the next section. If you are using some other kind of frame, you can start on any area you wish to do first.

When working edges, be sure to hook two rows of loops close together on all outside borders of a pattern. This tight, double row makes a firm edge that will wear well and will not open up to show backing when you hem or bind the finished rug.

WHERE TO START

As I have said, you can start hooking anyplace you want to. You can hook all the design first so as to try out different colors and see, as quickly as possible, how the finished design will look. Or if you are cautious you can work on the background only, while gaining experience and proficiency.

From experience, I have found that the best way lies between these two approaches. Hook some of the design first, outlining edges with a row of loops and then filling the center part. After completing a small section of the design, fill in some surrounding background. Hook the first row of background material close to the outline row of the design. By pressing background loops against the design, you can "set" a shape exactly as you want, the curve or point of a leaf or petal, for instance.

If you fill in background up close to the edges of a design, you may lose the outline of the design in the spread of the background material. Also, the effect of the design alone, hooked against the neutral color of rug backing, is sometimes deceptive, while an area of design with background filled close around it, shows clearly the effect of different colors in juxtaposition.

Colors blend more closely when hooked than they appear to do as cloth pieces, so, when you hook material into backing, you may lose expected contrast between colors in background and design. By hooking a small section of both together, you can sometimes spare yourself much ripping out if colors do not produce the desired results.

Finally, by hooking some design and then filling in some background, the rug progresses evenly. You avoid ending up with nothing but relatively unexciting background areas on which to work. For my own part, I enjoy the absorbing process of hooking design. Then I find it pleasant to do some background filling while I plan colors for another part of the design. Thus I tend to work from one end of a pattern to the other in rather steady fashion, even though tempted by an alluring section of design in a far corner of the rug. Of course, *you* should proceed exactly as suits *you* best. My own method is only a guarantee for me that all parts of a rug will be finished at about the same time.

XIX. SKIERS
Designed and hooked by Hans Vierling
A feeling of action produced by head-on figures and
touches of brilliant color.

XX. REX'S OCTAGON
32 by 56 inches
Edana Design
Hooked by Faye Kemp
A geometric in rich, muted colors.

XXI. MOTTO
18 by 36 inches
Designed and hooked by the author
Philosophizing in muted, home-dyed colors.

XXII. AMERICAN FANCY
34 by 44 inches
Designed by Heidi Gilmartin
Hooked by the author
An appealing mix of American needlecraft
motifs.

XXIV. MOSES
36 by 72 inches
Designed and hooked by Sue Whitman
Strong line and color give dignity and solidity
to this wall hanging.

XXIII. STAINED GLASS
14 by 72 inches
Designed and hooked by George Wells
Combines yarn and fabric in a close-color
harmony.

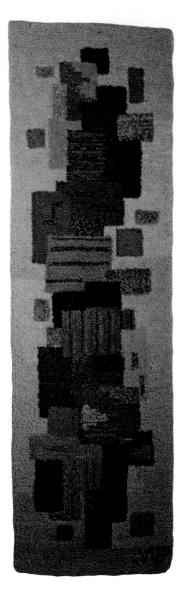

XXV. TEXTURED BLOCKS
22 by 60 inches
Designed and hooked by George Wells
Fine balance of different-size blocks and dark
and light color values.

XXVI. PINE TREE
36 by 70 inches
Designed by Heidi Gilmartin
Hooked by Jean Hersey
Stylized tree, outsize cones reproduced Jean's
charming idea of a pine tree.

CHAPTER 8

The Use of Color

How Can I Choose the Right Colors?

THERE are no "right" or "wrong" colors for hooking. However, those you select will determine to a great degree the character of your finished rug. A poor combination of colors can ruin a good design, while a well-chosen scheme will contribute to the beauty of a pattern. You should know something about color in order to use it effectively. You will want to understand the properties of each hue and the relationship of one to another when you are selecting from material you already have or dyeing fabric to suit your purpose.

THE SECRET OF COLOR HARMONY

Undoubtedly, you will be using more than one color in a rug, so you need to understand something of color harmony. Like separate notes in music that lose their identities in producing a beau-

tiful chord, so colors can be harmonized. In color, as in music, there are an infinite number of relationships.

Begin learning how to relate colors by observing and analyzing harmony wherever you see it. Try to separate the components that have produced a satisfying, aesthetic effect. You will soon realize how exciting color is and how it can be used to give pleasure and express feeling.

COLOR TERMS

If you familiarize yourself with a few terms used to describe color, it will make reading about color easier. As my purpose is to give simple instructions that will be helpful in planning a rug, I will not attempt to cover different theories of color measurement or to define terms other than the three essential ones. (If

69

you want more information, read one of the excellent books on color.)

These terms are the ones most generally used to describe color:

Hue refers to the name of a color, as red or blue. Each hue can be changed by mixing it with another. For example: red, mixed with yellow produces orange—a different hue.

Value refers to the degree of lightness or darkness in a hue. Thus, pink is a light value of red, and deep green a dark value of green. Dark values are sometimes called shades, and light values, tints. The value of a hue can be changed without altering the basic color. Use less color to get a lighter value. Use more for a dark value.

Intensity refers to the brilliance of a hue, whether it is bright or dull. In dyeing, intensity can be decreased by the addition of black or some dark color.

A COLOR WHEEL

A color wheel will help you learn about color. You can buy one at an art-supply store. On the wheel are shown the basic hues, from which all relationships and combinations are derived. Of first importance are the basic colors, from which all others can be mixed. Red, yellow, and blue are called *Primary Colors.*

The Secondary Colors lie between the primaries on a color wheel and are obtained by mixing two primaries. For instance: Equal proportions of red and yellow produce orange; of yellow and blue make green; of red and blue, violet. Thus, orange, green and violet are secondary colors. It is possible to get a range of shades in secondaries by varying the

proportions of primaries in the mixture.

Tertiary Colors are produced by mixing primary and secondary colors. In naming them, the primary color is set first, thus placing the tertiary in its specific family. For example: the tertiaries would be red-orange, yellow-green, blue-violet, yellow-orange, blue-green and red-violet.

RELATIONSHIPS OF COLOR

In their relationships, colors are considered as Complementary or Intermediate. This, too, is graphically depicted on a color wheel.

The primaries are called Complementary Colors. You will note that they lie directly opposite one another on the wheel. This is the key to their relationship, for opposed colors accentuate each other and tend to clash if used side by side.

The hues between primaries are called Intermediate Colors. You will see that they range from an intense hue nearest the primary to a neutral gray halfway between two primaries. Because of this range, their relationship is somewhat more complicated. Intermediate colors nearest the primaries are more intense, containing more of the primary. Intermediate colors will accentuate one another in direct proportion to the amount of primary color each contains. As they approach the center, between primaries, intermediates lose intensity to become grayed-out or neutralized. Neutral colors will neither intensify nor clash with either of the opposing primaries.

One of the odd facts about color is that neutral hues are obtained by a mixture of opposites. For instance, red mixed with green will make gray. And the range of intermediate colors is obtained by varying the proportions of the complementaries, thus bringing a color closer to one or the other of the primaries.

Through their relationships, colors contrast or harmonize with one another. This is the important fact in selecting hues for a rug. For harmony, you can use colors that are related through one predominating primary. For instance, all greens, whether yellow-green, blue-green or gray-green, go well together. You can use complementary colors for contrast, a bit of red in a rug that uses green as the main hue, or a dash of yellow in a rug that is predominantly blue. Finally, you can have any degree of harmony or contrast by varying the amount of the primary in the colors you select.

LIVING COLOR

Colors can do more than just harmonize or contrast, they can create mood. Colors affect our feelings, stimulating or soothing us. Indeed, they seem to have a life of their own, as some stand out and attract attention while others are quiet and retiring. Though individual response differs, certain hues nearly always seem lively and exciting and others restful and soothing. This being the case, colors are often classified as warm or cool.

Warm colors are those which are generally considered to be bold and advancing—reds, oranges, and yellows. Cool colors are those which are thought of as submissive and retreating as the various shades of blue or green.

Of course, the warm or cool effect of a color is in direct proportion to the de-gree of intensity. A bright orange or red will stimulate more than a muted tone of either. And neutral hues, as they contain equal proportions of both warm and cool color, evoke little response.

COLORS IN A RUG

Using color effectively in your rug-work, you can have either warm or cool colors predominate. For harmony, you can choose colors that go well together, and you can select the right hue for contrast.

Once you have decided on colors, you can plan how to distribute them, for a well-balanced color scheme is important in a rug.

For good balance, apportion colors in both area and intensity. You can equalize the amount of one color with the intensity of another. Then, if you want to emphasize a color, either use a large amount of a muted color or a small amount but of great brilliance. Thus your background could be light primrose yellow, or on a neutral background you could introduce small areas of intense gold or orange (red-yellow).

A standard "safe" distribution is to place neutral color in the largest area, usually the background, intermediate hues of slightly increased intensity in the next largest section and an intense color, or a contrasting one, in the smallest part of the rug.

You might decide upon a gray-green background, olive-green (a somewhat grayed yellow-green) for fairly large areas with accents of chartreuse (brilliant yellow-green) or of contrasting warm brown.

DEFINITE COLOR SCHEMES

There are several, definite color schemes that can be used for rugs. The easiest, and one that is often employed in textile work, employs just two colors. Blue, green, red, or gold on tan, white, gray or black makes a striking rug.

A monochromatic color plan is easy with only one color but in different values. This is a good scheme when color is intended to be subordinate to design, but to be effective, shades must contrast sufficiently, as pink and red or tan and brown.

An analogous color scheme is excellent for a rug. It employs several colors that have a common element, such as orange, green, and yellow. As these are closely related, they harmonize. To keep this scheme from being monotonous, it is a good idea to add a touch of color that is complementary to the dominant hue in the rug, as blue with the yellows.

An interesting, if somewhat tricky color scheme is the complementary one, with opposite colors producing "a harmony or contrast." With this plan, it is important to judge contrasts carefully. If they are too strong, a clash instead of harmony results. Avoid using complementaries in equal areas and in great intensities. Instead, fill a large area with one and a small area with another, as a quantity of red and a small amount of green. Or vary intensity, by using just a bit of bright red against a large area of grayed green.

No matter what the scheme, you can determine its special effect. If warm colors predominate, your rug will be gay and stimulating. If there are cool colors, your rug will be serene and restful.

THE ROOM AND THE RUG

You are aware that colors used together in a rug affect each other, that they harmonize or contrast. But perhaps you have not considered that colors in a rug affect those in the room in which it is placed.

If you do not know where a rug will be used, it is wise to select predominantly neutral hues. If you have decided on a location, it is important to choose the right colors for the desired effect of contrast or harmony with the setting.

It is not necessary to match color in a room to make a rug that harmonizes. It is more effective to have a rug with a different value of the main color in a room—a dark green rug in a room with light green walls, for instance. Or, you can use color in a rug that is similar in hue to the predominant color in the setting. A rug that contains yellow-gray, yellow-red, or yellow-orange will harmonize with a room say, with pale yellow walls. Less run-of-the-mill harmony is achieved by selective color for a rug that will be complementary to the main hue of a room, a soft shade of yellow in a blue room or a rug of grayed red in a green room.

To make a rug contrast with its setting, providing a decorative accent, select a color that contrasts strongly, either in intensity or value, with that in the room. A touch of blue is effective in a yellow room or a bit of intense red in a gray-green room.

Balance is important, too, between color in a rug and color in a room. A design of many hues or of brilliant hues is suitable for a predominantly neutral room. But in a setting that already has a fair amount of color in draperies or slipcovers it is best to make your rug fairly neutral.

CAUTION WITH COLOR

You will become excited by the possibilities of color and may want to use many hues in your first hooked rug. However, it is a fact that, in rugs, artistic results are more often achieved with a limited number and variety of hues. So, use caution with color, especially if color work is new to you. Do make the most of colors you select, by spreading them out freely rather than breaking them up into small spots.

WAYS TO SELECT COLORS

Now for some practical ways to select color for your rug. Of course, you can just choose colors you like and hook them in combination pleasing to you. Certainly, you will enjoy working and living with colors chosen on this basis. Or, if you feel unsure of your taste in color, you can carry out a scheme that is already present in some feature of your home, as in a painting, a drapery or a wallpaper design

The best way to work is directly with colors before you start hooking them in a rug. You can experiment with watercolors or crayon and color the paper drawing of a design. If you prefer, make a mixture of dye and water, and with a small stiff brush, color a design already drawn on backing.

An especially good way to try out col-

ors is to work with colored paper or materials. Lay out pieces of paper on backing. Distribute them for balance in color and for contrast or harmony. In the same way, you can spread out pieces of yarn or fabric and so judge its effect of various colors together.

With fabrics, spread them out on the floor in the room where the rug will be placed, if you have chosen your location. Arrange colors in a way that you think looks well, then stand back and consider the composition. You will readily see the colors that do not contrast enough or which ones stand out too sharply. At this point, you can take away or add colors until you get the right effect. Finally, place the remaining colors within the circumference of the pattern and distribute amounts and intensities until you are satisfied with the balance.

I enjoy working with materials this way and find it really helpful. I like to leave the final lay-out of material undisturbed for a few days. Then, I can return to examine the color scheme, to be sure it is just what I intend and perhaps, if I want, add a bit more color as a finishing touch.

RUGS ON LOCATION

There is no better way to see just what colors can do than to study rugs in specific locations where the effect of living color is evident and creates a special mood. Here, too, is seen the contribution of design, since design can never be separated from color. So, let us take an imaginary tour, through the following illustrations, to see what a hobby can do for a home.

THE ENTRY OFFERS A WARM WELCOME

Come in and see the most important area, the entry. Colors in the rug are apt to be bright and gay, to give instantly a feeling of warmth and welcome. Design, also, says something—telling us whether the home is traditional or modern, formal or informal. As a rule, in entries a lot of color and of design are both acceptable, since usually there is relatively little decoration here to compete with a rug. *American Fancy*, Color Plate XXII, voices a warm welcome in traditional style. *Gabriel*, Color Plate II, says the same in modern fashion. *Springtime*, Color Plate IX, is a half round entry rug, perfect for a doorway because of its appealing design and vivid, warm colors.

THE STAIRWAY IS A SHOWCASE

Next comes the stairway, an ideal showcase for both color and design, for here, as in the entry, there is seldom much other decoration. Design dresses up and light colors brighten what might otherwise be a rather dull area.

In addition, the stair carpet can introduce our hosts to us by telling us of their special interests. It may depict hobbies, give the life-story of the family, show their interest in the past with historical motifs or in nature with a theme like that in *Parade of the Seasons*, Illustration 4. Besides being extremely decorative, this stair rug eliminates noise and reduces the need to redecorate frequently, due to constant scuffing of treads and risers. Even more important, the rug promotes safety, as there is far less likelihood of slipping on a carpet that is securely fastened down than on bare wood.

In the stair carpet, for safety's sake, there should be a definite visual break between risers and treads. This break serves both a practical and aesthetic purpose, for medium colors and a subdued, allover design on the treads do not show soil, nor will their design and color steal from the effect of the risers.

Of course, if you use single pieces on the treads instead of making continuous carpeting, practical colors are best. Also, each piece should be secured, well back against the riser, to prevent tripping.

As a bonus, stair carpeting is fun to hook as it offers frequent opportunity to change color and to work on many different designs.

THE LIVING ROOM SETS THE TONE

Now, let us enter the living room, usually the main room of the home where the rug sets the tone. If this setting is visible from the entryway, the rug may well carry out an impression already given. However if the room is formal, with fragile, fine furniture, and perhaps seldom used, the rug may be of an intricate, delicate design in soft pastels to contribute to the effect of elegance, perhaps a rug like *Summertime*, Color Plate XIV.

In a home where antiques are cherished, we may see a rug like *Caswell Fruit*, Color Plate XIII, a rug of warm, rich hues in a primitive design to suggest a bygone time. In a modern setting, the rug may be a bright accent of color in a stylized design.

No matter what the tone of the room,

if it is a much lived in family room and especially if the rug is large, care must be taken to use practical colors. Medium shades are used in the largest sections, as lint and crumbs show on dark shades and stains and dirt on light ones. The rug-maker wants her work to be enjoyed, not guarded.

THE DINING ROOM HAS A PURPOSE

The dining room is a place with a purpose, a room where family and friends gather to eat and visit. According to psychiatrists, colors can stimulate both appetite and conversation, so hues in this rug can be bright, warm and gay. The pattern may be bold, too. Since this room is used for only a few hours of the day, there is no fear that either brilliant color or bold design will become tiresome.

Motifs of a dining-room design may be taken from patterns in china and silver or inspired by food. Design and color can be planned according to the arrangement of furniture so that the most interesting parts of the rug will show around the table and not be hidden beneath it.

THE BEDROOM IS PERSONAL

The bedroom is the most personal room in a home. It is here that individual preferences can be expressed in color and design. For the main bedroom, I like quiet geometrics or delicate florals. But let us visit a child's room. In his very own place, a youngster can have colors he likes and a design he finds appealing. These need not conform to adult tastes.

Children like bright colors and a de-sign with special meaning. So, in this room, you see a rug with an amusing picture executed in posterlike hues, perhaps one that tells a familiar story like *Noah's Ark*, or *Lion and Lamb*, Color Plates VII and VIII respectively. Or you may find an intriguing design like *The Morgan*, Color Plate XVI. You will note that the rug-maker has selected a pattern that will not be outgrown, a design that appeals to a young child but one that will also be enjoyed as he gets older.

There is another bedroom to visit, the guest room or possibly grandmother's room. Here, the rug is cheerful and cozy, using traditional design and realistic color for an intimate homey effect. *Hearts and Flowers*, Color Plate XII will give pleasure to either a permanent or a temporary guest.

MORE ROOMS, MORE RUGS

Of course, there are more rooms in the house where hooked rugs can be used. In those associated with activity, as kitchen and playroom, bright colors, informal designs and interesting textures are appropriate. In this kind of room, indeed, in any room, a geometric rug is ideal. And besides being suited to various settings, geometrics are fun to plan and hook as they offer infinite possibilities in design, color and texture. Color Plate XXV shows a treatment of a geometric design. *Textured Blocks* is perfect for a modern setting.

Perhaps, as you return to your own home after this imaginary tour, you will be inspired by what you have seen to plan an exciting future of rugmaking to beautify your own particular rooms.

CHAPTER 9

Commercial and Home-Dyed Color

How Can I Obtain Special Colors?

You can use commercially-dyed material or dye fabrics at home to get colors you want for rug-work. Commercial color, whether in dark or light values, is intense and "solid." Used as is in a rug, it produces an effect of clear, sharp contrast. While this is good for designs that are stylized, softened hues are generally more suitable for all types of patterns. They are essential in realistic, shaded work.

Commercial colors do not combine readily with home-dyed colors, which are always less intense. So, it is best to use just one or the other to complete a given design. However, you can both alter intensity and change hues of commercially-dyed fabrics, to increase the range of color.

ALTERING INTENSITY OF COMMERCIAL COLOR

You can reduce the intensity of commercial color by bleaching. With various procedures you can remove just a little color to soften a hue, take out more color to lighten it, get rid of almost all the color and then redye. To remove just a little color, soak the material in warm water mixed with a teaspoon or so of detergent. To take out more color, simmer material on the stove with detergent, or use a commercial bleach instead of the detergent. Follow directions carefully as too strong a solution may weaken a fabric.

You may want to remove only some of the color from a large quantity of material, lightening all of it to a similar value.

76

To do this, use the same amount of material with the same measured proportions of water and detergent or bleach for each successive operation. Time the process, so that in the end the different lots will be bleached to the same degree.

When bleaching a great deal of material at one time, or when you are trying to remove much color, change the water in the bleach-bath frequently. A balance is created when the amount of color in the water equals that remaining in the material. At that point no further color will be drawn off until the fresh water is used.

Always rinse your material well after bleaching to remove detergent or other agent and to make sure that the color remaining in the fabric will not run. You may find that color has been removed unevenly and the material is mottled. Usually, this can be avoided by stirring during the bleaching process. However, even if the fabric is blotchy it can often be used effectively in a rug. Indeed, many hookers strive for uneven color since, when hooked, it gives interesting variation to background or design.

I have found that some colors bleach more readily than others. Most pale colors can be removed entirely, others are difficult despite the use of a strong bleach. So test small pieces of different colored materials for ease and degree of color removal.

CHANGING COMMERCIAL COLOR

You can change commercial color by redyeing material, deepen light hues or brighten faded ones by adding dye of the same color, reduce intensity of color by adding a small amount of the complementary color dye. For example: Purple dye will mute yellow material, orange will soften blue and red will tone down green. To neutralize too-bright tones, you can add a little brown or black dye.

These procedures, like bleaching, change value but do not alter hue. But by redyeing, you can actually change commercial color. To do this, follow the suggestions given in Chapter 8. Change a primary color by adding dye of its complement. Thus, red material with blue dye will become purple, and blue with yellow dye will be changed to green.

Relate clashing colors by dyeing them to a similar and satisfying hue, as blue dye over green, gray, and red will produce blue-green, blue-gray and purple, all colors that go together. Also, you can relate hues by dipping all in a dye-bath of one color, as reds, greens, and blues, all tinged with yellow, will be enough alike to harmonize. Or you can blend harsh values of one color with an overall dye. Thus, clashing greens can be dipped in a solution of olive-green dye.

DYEING MATERIALS AT HOME

I think home-dyeing is really the easiest way to get the many hues in different values and intensities that are so valuable in rug-work. As it is possible to dye any amount of a color, you can make a complete plan for a rug in advance. But perhaps you have tried dyeing fabrics at home, touching up slipcovers or draperies, and found it a somewhat painful process. The way hookers dye is quite different. Their method is fun, neither time-consuming, messy, nor difficult.

You will enjoy working with color and probably the process will teach you more about color than any amount of reading. Though you may make mistakes at first, unexpected results are often beautiful in a rug. In fact, by experimenting in a dye-pot, you may even produce hues so lovely that they inspire your color scheme.

A FAST, NEAT, EASY PROCESS

Beginners usually feel there is ample choice of colors for rugmaking in commercially-dyed materials. However, as your hooking progresses, you will surely want many shades or special colors that may be difficult to obtain. You might have to spend more time and energy shopping for these than you would in dyeing them yourself. In one morning at home, you can dye enough material, in the colors you want, for several weeks of hooking.

Home-dyeing is a neat, tidy business, satisfactory to the most orderly person. Since the process can be repeated at any time to get the same color, it is not necessary to work with large pans and great quantities either of dye or material. So, even in a small kitchen, it is easy to prepare for dyeing, work without mess, and clean up quickly afterward, as I do in my own small kitchen. (At the end of this chapter I explain my method.)

Dyeing is not difficult, and there is much available information for the beginner in pamphlets and books of instruction written especially for rugmakers. You can even buy pamphlets with formulas for the dyeing of specific colors and you can purchase samples of material that show the exact hue obtained by following a given recipe. The use of special dyes,

available in many colors and shades, makes it easy to produce the colors you want. One manufacturer, W. Cushing and Company, offers eighty-four different shades. You can either buy basic colors and mix these to get different hues or buy dye of the particular shade you want.

DYEING IS NOT WASTEFUL

Home-dyeing need not be wasteful, for if you produce colors you do not like, and do not want to work on at the moment, you can set them aside for re-dyeing in any of the several ways suggested for commercial colors. Material that has not dyed evenly enough for your purpose can be dyed later with a deep "covering" hue. Colors that have become muddy can be brightened with yellow dye.

Use large plastic bags for storing material that is not the right color for the rug on which you are working. Separate material and label one bag for fabrics to be redyed, one for those to be bleached, and one for colors you want for another rug or for hooking small gift articles.

Eventually you may have on hand a backlog of material that is partially covered with dye. This will prove invaluable for dyeing dark colors or related shades. Indeed, when you have accumulated a supply of dyed fabrics, you can plan a rug with those alone.

An easy way to do this is to separate colors, no matter what value or intensity, keeping together all those closest to green, to red, to yellow, and so forth. Put indeterminate hues in a separate heap. Then, dye all greens in a large amount of green dye, all reds in red dye, all indeterminate colors in any dark hue, as brown or black.

Now, you can make an effective rug, either by using varying shades of a single color or several related hues. Balance colors in a geometric design or spread them in flowing areas in an abstract pattern. The indeterminate hues, which have been dyed a dark color, can be used for borders, as a foil for neutral tones or as accents against light values. If you feel that a plan using shades of one color or of closely related hues is monotonous, you can dye just a bit of contrasting color and use it as a touch of brilliance to spark the scheme.

USEFUL MATERIALS FOR HOME DYEING

If you decide to dye colors at home, save or buy material that is especially easy to dye. Light colors are best for dyeing light shades, since a covering hue will not be affected by color already in the material. Tints dyed over white or cream-colored fabrics are clear and brilliant. Tints dyed over pastels of a different color may be slightly altered. For instance: Light tones dyed over pale gray material will be dulled by the gray already present.

Of course, when dyeing dark shades, the amount of cover dye is usually so great that commercial colors already in the material will not alter hue. So use darker material for dyeing deep tones.

For home dyeing, I buy beige woolen material in quantity. It gives me ease and freedom in planning color. Over this, I can dye light shades of any color without concern about alteration in hue due to the amount of commercial color in the fabric.

While tints are slightly muted by the brown dye present, I happen to prefer these to brilliant pastels.

I also use beige for dyeing either medium or dark tones. And I like to have a quantity on hand so that when I wish to repeat a color, I can dye over the same kind of material I used before. Finally, as I nearly always have one hooking project underway, and another in the planning stage, it is convenient to have plenty of material at hand.

MY EASY METHOD OF HOME DYEING

You will find there are almost as many methods of dyeing as there are hookers. You will discover also that with a little experience, you will develop a procedure that is, in part, your own. The important thing is to use a method that is effective for you in your situation. My own, which I will describe, happens to suit my temperament, color-expectations —and kitchen.

Usually, I limit a dyeing session to about two hours, knowing this will not be tiring and that within this time I can dye enough material for many hours of hooking. First, I dye some material for background because I like to decide on this color before dyeing others to go with it. I do not dye all the material for this large area in one morning, nor do I dye more of this color during successive sessions, which would be boring. But I do keep an exact record of my procedure in dyeing this important color since eventually I will need to repeat if I am to have enough of the same color to complete the background. (In the next chapter, I will give examples of good records.)

During the same morning, after dyeing material for the largest area, I dye fabric in a few other hues for the rug. I enjoy dyeing small amounts of several different colors so that I can begin to see how they will look together. However, I do not feel that I must dye, in one session, some of all the colors planned for a rug.

I lay out a piece of the dyed background material on the kitchen counter and as I dye other colors I place them against this. By doing so I can judge the effect of the hues in combination. If the colors are so close that I am not sure of adequate contrast, I may cut several strips of each and hook them into the backing, first some background color and then some other colors right beside it. In this final test, if colors blend too much, I redye them to deeper or more brilliant tones for stronger differentiation. If you prefer, you can reverse this procedure and dye colors for your design first, then a background hue to blend or contrast with them.

Perhaps it is well to state here that, for several reasons, home-dyeing is not an exact science. Ingredients in dye packages differ slightly from time to time, home measurements cannot be of laboratory exactness, and the chemical content of water used for dyeing sometimes changes.

As a result, while you can match colors closely, do not count on an exact match next time. Accept this fact and you will be spared much sorrow. Indeed, plan to take advantage of it, using variations effectively or dividing them strategically in a rug. In Chapter 5, several ways are suggested to spread slight variations in color evenly through a design.

THE IMPORTANCE OF LIMITED DYEING

No matter what method you use, it is important to dye only a small amount of material at one time. It is much easier to handle small amounts, and they do not require bulky equipment. Furthermore, by limiting the process, you will limit time wasted if you make mistakes, and your mistakes will naturally be of small size and quantity.

In rug-work, you seldom need a lot of one color except for the background, so there is no reason for dyeing in quantity. And when you do want a lot of one hue, you can repeat the procedure to obtain it. Also, since colors blend closely when hooked, it is best to dye small amounts of several and test these together before going on to dye a large amount.

Finally, most hookers anticipate with pleasure a few hours of dyeing, but will put off this process if it means long hours in the kitchen.

CHAPTER 10

Equipment and Instructions for Dyeing

Can You Tell Me Exactly How to Dye Colors?

BEFORE dyeing materials at home, it is important to have easy, exact instructions and detailed information on both equipment and procedure. I have tried to offer these by including here a complete list of the things I use and a step-by-step description of the procedure I follow.

NECESSARY EQUIPMENT

All the equipment necessary for home-dyeing is easily obtained and inexpensive. Probably, you already have on hand some of what is needed. For dyeing either fabric or yarn, I use the following:

One enamel pan, with cover, 4-quart size to serve as dye-pot. If you wish, you can use aluminum. I prefer enamel be-

cause it is easy to see into and judge how much dye has been absorbed by the material. I use a covered container in order to heat the water quickly.

One large container with cover in a size to fit your oven. This is used for steaming material to set color. Color can be set by boiling instead of steaming, but using the oven for this step lets me keep the top of the stove clear for more dyeing.

One enamel pan, 2- or 3-quart size. This is a side pan to place near the dye-pot. I fill it halfway with cold water for quick cooling of a test strip taken from the dye-pot when I want to see color and shade. Also, I carry in it a quantity of material taken from the dye-pot to the sink for cooling and rinsing. As with the dye-pot, I prefer an enamel pan because in enamel it is easier to tell whether or not the color is fast when rinsing the material.

A long-handled wooden fork with which to stir material in the dye-pot. Unlike metal a wooden handle will not get hot, and a fork is good for moving material about in thorough, rapid stirring.

A pair of tongs with which to transfer a quantity of dripping, hot fabric from dye-pot into side pan, without risk of its slipping and splashing back into the hot water. Tongs are useful, also, for picking out a single piece from the dye-pot to hold up for inspection of shade and color.

Several 2½-cup jars with screw-on lids. These are containers for the liquid dye mix. Size is important as there must be enough "head room" for thorough stirring of dyes, whether mixed with 1 or with 1½ cups of water. Furthermore, it is easy to dip spoonsful of liquid dye from a container of this size, but difficult to reach into a much larger jar. It is essential to have a tight lid, for the whole amount of liquid dye is seldom used in one session and the cover is needed to prevent evaporation during storage. Also, a tight cover will keep contents from spilling if the jar is tipped over inadvertently.

A box of small paste-on labels. Each jar should be labeled immediately after dye is mixed in it, for it is impossible to guess exact color from the appearance in the jar. Probably you will mix several different colors in one morning and you will doubtless store some of these, so it is important to know, when you use them next, what color each jar contains.

A teaspoon for stirring mixtures of dye and water. Empty a single package of dye into a jar, add the required amount of boiling water and stir well. Rinse the spoon before stirring a mixture of another color.

A measuring cup for measuring water into the jar and also for measuring mordant or dye-setter into the dye-bath. (Mordant will be discussed shortly.)

A set of metal measuring spoons to measure dye from jar into dye-pot. Dip the spoon holding the dye well into the hot water in the dye-pot, thus ensuring removal of all dye from the spoon. This will also rinse the spoon, important if you use it to dip out a dye of different color. I prefer metal to plastic spoons as plastic sometimes warps after repeated dipping in hot water.

A gallon or ½ gallon of white vinegar or a large quantity of uniodized salt. Either of these act as mordants, the agent which helps set dye in the material. You can use whichever you prefer and, of course, either will be less expensive if bought in quantity.

One package detergent or special "wetting-out" product. Material to be dyed is first thoroughly saturated or wetted out, as this is sometimes called, to help the dye penetrate more quickly and evenly. You can use a mixture of water with a few teaspoons of detergent or one of the commercial wetting-out products.

Six or more packages of dye, the colors for your work. Have on hand those you definitely plan to use, plus a few packages of complementary colors that may be needed for dulling too-bright hues. Also, it is a good idea to have a package of brown dye and one of black, as you may want to add a few drops of brown to soften brilliant colors or a little black to dull them. I keep an extensive file of dyes of different colors, in case I decide to add an "unplanned" one to the dye-bath. In addition, I like to use free moments to experiment with colors I have not previously tried.

A pair of rubber gloves. Commercial dyes, unless otherwise stated on the package, are not injurious to the skin but they do stain. I work more comfortably without gloves, since I know that most of the stain can be removed by scrubbing and, truthfully, I am not much concerned if my hands are slightly stained. However, you may be.

A full-length apron. Dyes will stain clothes and even the most careful worker sometimes drips or splashes. To protect clothes, wear a large apron and, if you wish, keep it just for use when dyeing. While I usually wear an apron, I confess that when I am eager to start dyeing, I sometimes forget it. As a result, I have several "dyeing outfits." When I do wear an apron, I am inclined to wipe my hands on it during dyeing, and so mine is now a garment of rainbow hues.

Material. Get together all you intend to use during one morning of dyeing. In fact, it is wise to put out more than you expect to use. When working for a color you have not dyed before, you may not succeed with the first batch of material and so will need extra to continue dyeing. Also, if you finish dyeing sooner than expected, you may want to go ahead and dye more.

Stove. This is essential equipment for home-dyeing, since heat is an important factor in setting dye in fabric.

Notebook and pencil. The final necessity for home-dyeing. This is so important that I will discuss it at length.

THE IMPORTANT RECORD BOOK

A complete record of dyeing procedures is invaluable to a rugmaker, for it ensures against error when repeating a color and provides inspiration and instruction for other workers too.

In your notebook you will write the formula for achieving a color. This formula is a listing of proportions of dye to material to dye-bath. It includes a description of the kind of dye and type of material used, and to be complete, the name of the rug for which the colors were mixed.

Not including specific amounts of dye, which I will discuss shortly, your record might appear thus:

EAGLE RUG

Beige wool, purchased at Smith's Rug Shop

Dyed as a single group: 10 strips measuring 3 by 12 inches

Cushing's Perfection Dye, "Olive Green"

Dye-bath: 3 quarts water to ½ cup vinegar. (If you always use same proportions in dye-bath, simply note "usual dye-bath.")

Dyed 4 shades, for olive branch and border

You should record, too, your exact procedure, for you may not always follow the same method, and a change may alter proportions. These notes might read as follows:

(1) Changed water in dye-pot each time I dyed more material.

(2) Added water to dye-pot, bringing

up to same level before each dyeing operation, or

(3) Added no water to dye-pot during entire process.

To make a record book especially interesting, staple or paste small samples of dyed material beside each formula. You can even paste a color picture of the finished rug following formulas used for it. You will profit by looking at this, noting colors that look perfect and those that are not quite so successful. Thus, your notebook can be a stepping-stone to color-planning your next rug.

It is wise to jot down all formulas that produce colors you like, even though these are not right for the rug on which you are working. You may want to repeat these hues sometime for another rug. Record color failures, too, to help avoid wasting time by mixing the same combination of dyes again.

Use a section of your notebook for pieces of fabric and samples of color like those provided by paint companies. Paste in anything you find that has color combinations you find pleasing. This section of your notebook will be an invaluable inspiration and guide in dyeing.

CHANGING PROPORTIONS

In home-dyeing, proportions are the main consideration, for as these change, so do the rate of absorption and the final results. To understand this, imagine that you are changing proportions as follows:

First, change proportions of dye. Assume that you are using three quarts of water to ten 3- by 12-inch strips of material to one teaspoon of liquid dye. This is rather a large amount of material to a small amount of dye and, as a result, the dye will be absorbed quickly. Now, use the same amount of material and water and increase the proportions of dye to several tablespoons. This larger amount will take longer to absorb. *Thus a small amount of dye is taken up more quickly than a large amount.*

Next, change proportions of material. Use 3 quarts of water, 1 teaspoon of dye and just a few strips of material. It will take several minutes for this small amount of material to absorb the dye. Now, use about 10 strips. Dye will be absorbed almost instantly. *Thus a large amount of material absorbs dye more quickly than a small amount.*

Finally, change the proportions of water. Once again, use 10 strips of material to 1 teaspoon of dye, but only 1 quart of water. It will take some time for the color to absorb. Now, use the same proportions of material and dye to 5 or 6 quarts of water. Color will be absorbed quickly. *Thus in a strong solution with a small amount of water, dye is not absorbed as quickly as in a weak solution, which uses a large amount of water.*

Proportions of mordant to water must also be considered. While a mordant helps material absorb dye, it does not affect color, so there is no harm in using a lot. But the amount of mordant in the water will hasten absorption only to a certain point; beyond that, it is wasteful to add more. For 3 quarts of water, ½ cup of vinegar or uniodized salt is sufficient.

Heat is the final element to consider in home-dyeing. A certain amount is needed to set colors quickly, more to set them permanently. For quick absorption of color, a dye-bath should be almost at boiling. But, except when using a large amount of dye for especially dark colors, it is not necessary actually to boil fabric. For setting colors permanently, you can either simmer material on the stove or steam it in the oven.

At the risk of being repetitious but with the hope of saving you some time, I include a few more pointers. When dyeing dark shades, those requiring a large amount of dye, some color may remain in the bath even after simmering material for 10 or 15 minutes. This does not mean you must change water each time you dye dark shades of the same hue. But, if you proceed to dye light shades, start with clear water. Otherwise colors will be deepened or altered, depending on the color of the dye remaining in the bath.

When dyeing for light shades, requiring little dye, you will find that water in the dye-bath will remain clear through several successive operations. However, as you continue using the same water for dyeing several batches of material, the level will gradually be lowered. As the proportion of water decreases, the strength of the dye-bath will increase, so that shades dyed last will be darker than those dyed first.

STEP-BY-STEP PREPARATION

Step by step, this is the way I prepare for a dyeing session. While the description may seem lengthy, you will find that it takes only a little time to get everything ready.

1. Prepare material. If using yarn, tie about 10 yards in a loose hank; if using material, tear into short, wide strips, about 3 by 12 inches. Then, fill the sink with enough warm water to cover the material and add about 2 teaspoons of detergent or the prescribed amount of wetting-out product. Move the material about until it is thoroughly saturated.

2. Remove and wring out together the number of strips to be dyed as a group.

3. Place each twisted group on the counter. Proceed until all material has been wrung out in this way. (You need not rinse the material unless you used too much detergent, making it so soapy that suds rise in the dye-pot and it is hard to see the absorption of dye.

4. Fill a pint pan with water, cover and place on the stove to heat for use in mixing dyes.

5. Spread newspaper on the kitchen counter near the stove.

6. Place on the newspaper all the equipment: the jar of vinegar, dye jars and teaspoon, packages of dye, measuring cup and measuring spoons, wooden fork, tongs, labels, notebook and pencil.

7. Prepare the dye-bath by filling the 4-quart pan with 3 quarts of water and ½ cup of vinegar. Cover the pan and put it on the stove to heat.

8. Place a side pan, half filled with cold water, beside the dye-pot.

9. Fill a pitcher with hot water and set this near the dye-pot, so that you can add water to the bath, if necessary, as work progresses.

10. Mix the dyes. Empty a package of dry dye into a jar, label as to kind of dye and color. Add a prescribed amount of the hot water. Stir well and cap tightly. Rinse the teaspoon. Mix the other packages of dye in the same way.

11. Remove the cover from the dye-

pot. At this point the water should be hot but not boiling. It may be necessary to lower the heat just enough to keep the water from boiling and still ensure that it stays hot enough to set colors quickly.

At last, you are ready to dye and, as it is easiest to work with only one color, I will describe, first, the procedure for dyeing several shades of a single color.

DYEING SHADES OF ONE COLOR

This procedure is based on dyeing five 3- by 12-inch strips of woolen material as a single group. Dye the lightest shade first. This can be darkened easily, if you wish, but dark tones are not easily lightened.

FOR THE LIGHTEST SHADE:

1. Put ½ teaspoon liquid dye into the dye-pot. Stir well. Shake out twisted group of strips and plunge them all into the bath at once. Stir immediately and thoroughly until water is clear.

2. With tongs, remove all material to the side pan, holding it above the dye-pot to drip for a moment before transferring.

3. Wring out the material.

4. Straighten each strip and lay it on the counter.

5. Write Shade I in your notebook and record the amount of dye used to obtain it.

FOR SHADE II, THE NEXT DARKEST:

1. Add water from the pitcher to the dye-pot, bringing the level up to the original 3 quarts. This step may not be necessary yet, as you have dyed only one small group and so removed only a little water. You can judge accurately either by using a pot that has measurements marked on the side, or by chipping the enamel a little at the 3 quart level, as I have done with mine.

2. Add some vinegar to replace that used in dyeing the first group of strips. Since only a small amount has been removed, you can replace it by tipping in just a little vinegar directly from the bottle.

3. Add 1½ teaspoons of dye to the pot. Follow the same procedure as for Shade I.

4. Continue dyeing successive groups, increasing the dye each time to three times the amount used for the previous shade. An increase of three in dye proportions usually produces shades that are quite close, but adequately differentiated. But, if shades seem too close, increase the "jump" in proportions. (If now, or at some future time, you want to dye more of just one shade, you can do so by using the amount of dye specified in the formula for this particular shade.)

When you have dyed four or five shades, progressing from light to dark, you will reach a point where you are working for an extremely dark tone. By this time, you will probably be using several tablespoons of dye. Instead of continuing to increase the amount of dye of one color, try adding a small amount of dye of a complementary color to increase depth. Often, a color can be darkened more quickly by adding 1 or 2 teaspoons of its complement than by increasing quantities of the same color. And, the small amount of "different" color will not alter the main hue, the one that contains a much larger amount of dye.

5. When you have finished dyeing the required number of shades, place all strips in the steaming pan and add enough water to cover the bottom of this container.

6. Set the oven for medium heat, about 350 degrees, and steam the material for 20 minutes.

7. Finally, hang or spread strips out to dry. Sometimes, I use an electric clothes dryer to dry material quickly. So far it has never hardened or shrunk the dyed material.

After the dyeing of five shades of Olive-Green, the formula in your notebook might appear thus:

Shade I...½ teaspoon Olive-Green
Shade II...1½ teaspoons Olive-Green
Shade III..4 teaspoons Olive-Green
Shade IV..3 tablespoons Olive-Green
Shade V...3 tablespoons Olive-Green
             1 teaspoon Cardinal Red

WORKING WITH MORE THAN ONE COLOR

It is an easy step from dyeing shades of one color to mixing several different colors for a variety of hues. You can mix liquid dyes in a dye bath just as you might combine colors on a palette, adding amounts of several colors before putting in the material. Or, you can dye material with one color, remove the fabric from the bath, add another color, and then replace the material to dye the second color over the first. Once you get a color you like by mixing different dyes, you can proceed to dye several shades of it. Simply increase the proportions of dye in the same way as for shades of one hue.

First, try mixing just two colors. Put 3 teaspoons of red and 1 teaspoon of yellow in the dye-pot. Then put in your material. This combination will produce a brilliant scarlet.

Or use a large amount of brown with a small quantity of yellow to dye one group of strips. Or combine a large amount of brown with a small quantity of red for a second group. Thus you will produce two quite different shades of brown.

By mixing equal proportions of black and green, you can get "antique black," a color dear to hookers reproducing old rugs. Indeed, there are endless combinations of two colors that will produce beautiful hues, so try several and *keep a record of results*.

Now try three or more colors together to dye a group of strips. This is where the fun of home-dyeing really begins, for you can get an infinite number of colors by varying combinations and proportions. You will see that hues resulting from a mixture of several colors have depth and sparkle beyond hues of just one color. While you may produce some ugly colors in this venture, there is a better than even chance that you will get some astonishingly beautiful ones.

You can be bold or cautious in your approach to dyeing with several colors. To be bold, put an amount of each color into the dye bath, stir and then add material. To be cautious, dye a group of strips in one color, then remove the material to the side pan. Add a second color to the bath and return the strips so as to put this hue on top of the first. Repeat the process of removing material between each addition of a new color. With the cautious approach, you can stop at any point. With the bold one, you are wholly committed to the results of one combination.

By whichever method you dye with several colors, you can test color with a small piece of material before putting in the whole group of strips. For this, tear off a 2- or 3-inch piece of material. Holding it with tongs, swish it through the dyebath. Color on this test piece will not be exactly like that on a group of strips, since the amount of material is small in relation to what will actually be used. But the test piece will give a good indication of the kind of color resulting from your combination of dyes.

You can test with just one color in the bath by laying the test piece aside on the counter. Then add another color to the dye-pot and test again with another small piece of material. By doing this each time you add a different color, you can judge by test pieces the direction in which your combination of dyes is leading. When you are satisfied with the results on a small piece, you can go ahead and dye a group of strips.

Again, keep a record of amounts and colors of dye used for your good combination. Then you can repeat it just by putting the specified amounts together in the dye-pot. You won't have to go through the process of working toward the color a second time.

It is well worth while to spend a morning in this kind of experimentation, for it is one of the easiest, most interesting ways to learn how colors go together. Though you may waste some material, you will also lose your inhibitions about combining hues.

Here is a sample formula using 4 different colors to produce a warm, lively red:

1 tablespoon Turkey-Red
2 teaspoons Cardinal-Red
1 teaspoon Canary-Yellow
⅓ teaspoon Dark-Green

DYEING TRICKS FOR SPECIAL EFFECTS

You will probably discover a few dyeing "tricks" for obtaining special effects. Here are some that other hookers have invented and that you may enjoy trying.

To mottle material, do not saturate it before dyeing. Then color will be absorbed unevenly. For the same purpose, crowd more material into the dye-pot than it can easily contain, so that some parts will be in closer contact with the dye solution than others and will thus absorb more color.

To mottle material in more than one color, put a large amount of fabric in the dye-pot with only 1 to 2 inches of water. Either drip a little liquid dye or sprinkle a bit of dry dye onto the material. Then, turn over the whole heap, sprinkle with another color, and continuing thus, use several different hues. This will produce a rainbow effect on strips.

You can obtain similar results by laying out strips, wet or dry, on a counter and sprinkling a different color of liquid or dry dye on each one. Then roll each strip, like a jelly roll, lay them in the dye-pot with just enough water to cover the bottom, and steam. Steam will dissolve the dyes and cause them to spread and flow together.

To get several shades quickly, put a few teaspoons of dye in the pot, then all the material to be dyed. Stir for just a moment, then remove some of the strips. Continue stirring the rest for a short time, then remove a few more. Stir the strips left in the pot until the small amount of dye still in the bath is absorbed. You will produce three shades, the darkest material that which was left in the longest.

Obviously, with this procedure you will not produce shades that are exactly differentiated, nor shades that can be repeated, since the proportions are constantly changing and an element of time is involved. However, it is a really fast way to get several shades and, in rugwork, it is not always necessary to have carefully-gradated tones or to repeat any one.

To dye three shades on the same group of strips, first put a few teaspoons of dye into the pot. Shake out a group of strips and hold these at one end with tongs. Dip the other end into the bath, to about one-third the length of the strips. Hold there for a short time, then lower the strips into the bath so they are covered to two-thirds their length. Hold them at this level for a while, then drop them into the pot. Stir until the dye left in the bath is absorbed.

These strips will be dark on one end, the end that was put into the bath first and so was in contact with the strongest dye solution. The middle section will be a medium shade and the other end light.

Shaded strips are sometimes used for hooking flowers. Since 3 inches of material, when hooked, makes about 1 inch of loops, a petal that is about 3 inches long can be shaded easily from light to dark with such a strip. Shaded strips can also be used for making a subtly-shaded border on a rug, starting at the outside edge of the rug with the darkest end of the strip and working toward the center of the rug to the lightest end. In similar fashion, shaded strips can be used to shadow around a center design starting at the edges of the design with the dark end of the strip and working outward to the light end.

These are just a few of the many dyeing procedures that have been developed by rugmakers. Try using those procedures that appeal to you. Then go ahead and invent some of your own. You will find that by experimenting freely and fearlessly in home-dyeing you can make your kitchen a color world of excitement and pleasure.

CHAPTER 11

Finishing and Care of Rugs

Does a Hooked Rug Need Special Care?

W<small>HEN</small> you have finished hooking a rug, you can either hem or bind the edges. Binding is essential for a strong edge if you have used burlap as a foundation, because threads of this fabric are not pliable and tend to wear out if folded. If you have used monks cloth, which is pliable, you need only hem the edges of a finished rug.

Many hookers bind a pattern before hooking it. With this method, rug-tape is machine-stitched on all edges. Then the outside rows of loops are hooked up close to the tape. When the rug is completed, the tape is turned back and stitched against the under side. No part of the binding shows on the surface of the pattern.

I prefer to bind edges after the hooking is completed. Tape is stitched through the outside row of loops and, when turned back over this thickness for final sewing on the underside, ¼ inch of binding remains on the upper surface. This small amount of tape on the top makes a firm edge just where a rug is most apt to wear out. Since tape is available in different colors, or can easily be dyed to match the background of a rug, I do not think the bit of tape that is visible is objectionable.

BINDING A RUG

To bind a rug, first trim the backing to about ¾ inch from the hooked edge. Lay the cotton rug tape on the right side of rug with the outer edge of tape even with the outside row of loops. Using heavy cotton or linen thread and sewing with either a close overcast or button-hole stitch, fasten these together firmly. Sew right through the outside row of loops, about ⅛ inch in from the edge of the tape.

Next, turn the binding back evenly onto the underside of the rug, pin the binding in place and sew it down with wide overcast stitches. Be careful not to pull the thread so tight that the edges are gathered up. You can prevent this by rolling the edge over your hand to keep it stretched as you sew.

To bind a round or oval rug, use bias tape. Since this is not available in an adequate width for a rug, you will have to make your own. To do this, use any heavy cotton material, first dyeing it to match the background of the rug, if you wish. Fold the material on the bias and cut several strips about 2 inches wide. Stitch these together to make a length that will go around the edges of the pattern. Then, following the same procedure used to bind straight edges, stitch this tape to the rug, stretching it at the corners to lie evenly.

HEMMING A RUG

To hem a rug, first trim material at the edges to make an even margin of about 2 inches. Next, fold the raw edge toward the back of the rug, up to the outside row of hooking. Then, fold again onto the under surface, pressing the fold back firmly from the hooked edge so that no foundation fabric will show from the top. Pin this hem down at intervals to hold it in place, cutting away excess material at the corners to make flat, mitered folds.

Use heavy cotton or linen thread and sew with widely-spaced overcast stitches.

Here again, do not pull stitches so tight that the edge is drawn up.

A FINAL, PROFESSIONAL TOUCH

Pressing a rug is a final, professional touch which serves to flatten out edges and uneven loops and make the surface absolutely smooth.

To press a rug, lay it face down on an ironing board, or if the rug is too large for this, place it on layers of newspaper on the floor. Then, wet a large piece of heavy cotton cloth, wring it out well and spread it over the rug. Press over this with a hot iron. If you are steaming a large rug, you may need to wet the pressing cloth several times as it becomes dried by the iron. Go over the surface of the pattern in the same way. Then, lay the rug out flat so that it can dry thoroughly before you use it.

THE BEST OF CARE

Since you will have put much time, energy and thought into making your rug, you will want to give it the best of care. This is easy.

Regular, gentle cleaning is the best way to ensure long rug wear, as it removes particles of dirt that might be ground in and eventually weaken the fabric. Remove spots as soon as possible, using water for non-greasy ones and dry-cleaning fluid for tar or grease. Vacuum the surface just as you do other carpeting. Occasionally, perhaps once a month, vacuum the under side as well. Or, you can safely clean a hooked rug by sweeping it. This is especially effective for rugs of varying loop heights that are not easily vacuumed.

If a rug is quite soiled, use a commercial dry-cleaning product to renew the colors. For a light cleaning, any of the powder types are good. I use Glamorene, a moist powder, sold in jars. To clean a rug with this, spread a handful of the powder thinly over the surface. Then, brush the powder in lightly with a broom or stiff brush, leave it until it dries and then vacuum the rug.

Shampooing is an equally effective way to clean and brighten a rug. Use mild soap and a soft brush and use suds only so as not to get the rug too wet. Brush in a large circle, then wipe with a damp towel or sponge to remove the dirt. Now clean a second area, overlapping the first. There are several good commercial shampoos, all with complete directions or, if you prefer, you can use any mild soap to make suds.

If a rug becomes really dirty, or if you want to give it an especially good cleaning, perhaps for an exhibit or a photograph, you can clean it more vigorously. Since a well-hooked rug is fairly tough, it can stand occasional rough treatment. While some hookers may frown at my method here, it has not harmed my rugs and has served to restore much-used ones to almost original freshness.

For this thorough cleaning, I use Liquid Glamorene, mixing it in a pan with water as directed, and I fill a second container with warm water. Then, I dip a scrub brush into the cleaning mixture and scrub a small area of the surface vigorously. After this, I wring out a small turkish towel in the clear water and wipe off this area. I proceed, in this way, to wash the whole rug, changing rinse water from time to time as it becomes dirty. After shampooing, I allow the rug to dry thoroughly before using it.

REPAIRING RUGS

Occasionally, a hooked rug needs repair, owing to damage wrought by prolonged hard usage or perhaps by household pets.

To repair a worn or pulled area, first remove loops all around the damaged spot. Then, sew a new piece of foundation fabric onto the back of the rug, under the area to be rehooked. This piece should be large enough to extend at least 1 inch beyond the section to be repaired. Now, hook loops to fill, using as many strips as you can salvage from the edges of the worn spot and mixing these with new strips that match as closely as possible.

If the edge of a rug wears out, remove the old binding and replace with new. Set new tape back slightly from the worn edge. If a rug is hemmed, you can undo the old hem, turn it back farther and restitch. However, in case a hemmed edge wears out, it is probably better to bind to add durability to the edge.

Incidentally, once you have learned how to hook, you may find you are able to repair machine-made rugs as well as hand-hooked ones. For this, use short strips of material or yarn, depending on the type of material originally used in the rug. Hook in new loops, cutting or leaving uncut according to the surface. I have repaired sections of my own and my neighbor's machine-made rugs that have been damaged by pets, by rehooking pulled-out strips into the backing.

IMPORTANCE OF PADDING

For several reasons, all rugs should be laid over a pad. For one, it is safer, keeping a rug from skidding out from under foot. Also, a pad will make a rug wear longer and, finally, it will make it feel softer to walk on.

You can use thin sheets of foam rubber for padding and this can be cut with ordinary household scissors. Cut it about ½ inch smaller than the outside measurements of the rug. Or, if you prefer, you can use a heavier commercial padding, such as Ozite.

However, padding will not always keep a rug from slipping. So, it must be remembered that any small rug can be dangerous in certain areas of the home. A rug placed at the head of stairs, for instance, should be tacked down to prevent skidding.

RUG SIZING

There are various commercial products for coating the underside of a rug. Spread on or sprayed on, they serve to cement loops firmly to the backing, and some are advertised to preventing skidding as well. A well-packed rug of uncut loops does not require sizing, nor is it essential for one of cut loops if these are closely hooked.

STORING AND CARRYING

Clean a rug thoroughly and spray with a moth-preventive before storing it. Then use plastic bags, newspapers or wrapping paper, to cover it. If possible, lay a rug flat for storage, if not, roll it with the top surface on the outside. Never fold or roll a rug outside in, because this stretches fibers of the foundation fabric, weakening them and perhaps causing a break.

For rolling a large rug, the heavy cardboard tubes used by carpetmakers are useful. Or your rug can be rolled over a bamboo pole or over a large roll of newspapers.

INSURING A RUG

The only additional care you can give a rug is to insure it. A rug that is well made can be insured for its market, if not its personal value. Even though a hand-hooked rug is irreplaceable, some compensation in case of loss lightens the tragedy.

CHAPTER 12

More Hooking Projects

Can I Hook Something Besides a Rug?

THE fun of hooking need not begin or end with a rug, for there are many other hooked articles that are interesting to make. And these can be both decorative and practical, useful to own, to give away or to sell. You can make a wall hanging, a picture, a pillow top, chair seat, pocketbook, doorstop, mat or set of coasters. Any of these projects can be finished quickly, and all offer a fine chance to try out ideas of design and color.

WALL HANGINGS AND PICTURES

A hanging, whether large or small, can have great decorative impact and so should be carefully planned to blend or contrast with a setting. A bold design in vivid colors will be just right in one room, a delicate, soft-hued pattern appropriate to another. The hanging, *Moses,* Color Plate XXIV, is perfect for the place where it is used, a wide hallway in a modern, Jewish synagogue. Since it is the only decoration in this spacious setting, strong lines and color are demanded for dramatic effect.

In most homes, smaller hangings of subdued design and color are best. If you like, you can draw a design that is appropriate, or you can select a commercial one. You may find a pattern for a rug that is suitable, as many of these are adaptable for use as wall pieces. *Textured Blocks,* Color Plate XXV, is a fine example.

If you would rather make a picture than a hanging, you can also choose from many commercial designs. Or draw one yourself that is individual and especially suited for your room. You might enjoy hooking a scenic pattern, a vista of mountains and lakes, a rugged seacoast, a garden or a winter scene, as in *In the*

Meadow, Color Plate XV. Just as interesting to make would be a picture of the family homestead, a village or farm scene, perhaps in the style of, but not copied from, Grandma Moses, or one of the Currier and Ives prints.

Indeed, an almost endless variety of subjects can be used effectively as hooked pictures. Flower designs are attractive, formal bouquets or loose arrangements of a few leaves and blossoms. Flowers, fruit, leaves or seed pods, arranged like a botanical print, can be used as single pictures or planned as a series. Equally enjoyable to hook and as decorative are pictures of birds, butterflies, insects or fish. Maps or coats-of-arms also make handsome designs. Hobbies suggest motifs —horses, trains, antique cars, dolls or soldiers—to be done in realistic colors or in silhouette fashion.

As a quaint touch, sentimental verse can serve as the basis for a hooked picture, perhaps one that commemorates a wedding or anniversary. A portrait is fun to do, one of the family pet, a member of the household or a nostalgic picture.

A hooked picture, like any other kind, should be properly framed. Style, size and color of a frame will contribute to setting off a pattern. It is important to have a frame large enough to carry the amount of color and design.

Usually, a heavy, wide frame is best for a large, intricate design, while a narrow band may be all that is required for a small, delicate pattern. The color of the frame should contrast sufficiently with the color of the background of the picture. Often, a bit of color in the frame will accentuate a particular hue in the pattern. The type of frame can be related to the idea of the picture. An abstract design looks best in a simple, flat frame, a Victorian piece in an ornate, carved one and a small scenic design or stylized fruit or flower motif is effectively set off by a shadow-box frame.

USEFUL SMALL ARTICLES

It is pleasant to make small hooked articles, pillow tops, chair seats, stool covers, pocketbooks, doorstops, mats, or coasters. There are commercial designs for all of these or, since almost any subject is suitable, you can draw your own design easily. Flower, fruit, animal or bird motifs are appropriate. So are geometric patterns, and these can be made to fit either modern or traditional interiors by the special use of color.

Pillow tops, chair seats and stool covers can be made in various sizes and shapes, thus solving the problem of covering an odd-shaped piece of furniture. Pocketbooks, too, can be made in any size, from a small "clutch" purse to a large "tote" bag. Doorstops, mats, and coasters, the smallest of all hooking projects, are often the most fun to make, the most marketable and the most welcome as gifts. And a special small item, hooked rugs for doll houses, delights worker and recipient.

CHAIR SEATS, PILLOW TOPS, AND STOOL COVERS

In a design for a pillow top, chair seat, or stool, motifs should be arranged to suit the shape and their size should be in keeping with size of the piece. A central figure or group is excellent in a circular piece, with enough area around the drawing for balance. A design that follows the contours of the pillow, chair seat or stool is equally good, as for example a wreath of fruit or flowers.

For any size and shape, geometric or repeat designs are effective. Squares, circles or diamonds can be hooked in brilliant hues for a modern piece or in muted tones for an antique. And any small motif can be repeated, either in ordered rows and blocks or as a scattered design.

Use bias tape to bind the edges of a chair seat and back it with felt or other material for neatness and added thickness. You can secure the pad to the chair by using small ties sewed at the corners of the cushion. Or cut a piece of thin foam rubber and place it underneath the pad to keep it from slipping.

A hooked pillow top can be used for either a box or a plain pillow. For the back of the pillow, select a fabric that is suited to the design and one that carries out the color scheme. Velvet is lovely for delicate, realistic flower patterns and corduroy or cotton is fine for either modern or traditional designs and colors.

MATS AND COASTERS

You can make mats of any size. You can easily hook a square or rectangular mat or, by drawing around a saucer, dinner plate or platter, make a circular or oval mat. Mats are placed under hot tea or coffee pots or under hot serving dishes. Between times, they can be hung on small hooks to decorate kitchen or dining room.

Usually, a small design is all that is needed for a mat, perhaps a bunch of grapes or cherries, or a delicate small cluster of bright blossoms as in the square

mat shown in Color Plate IX. A pattern of vegetables would be just as suitable, and for a more formal piece, a single blossom or a spray of flowers. It is fun to make a series of mats in different sizes and shapes but with related motifs for design, as different fruits, flowers or birds.

Hooked coasters are practical and decorative, and a set of four or six can be made rather quickly. You can use the same figure in each mat and just change colors to make them slightly different. Or carry out a theme, perhaps a nature one with mushroom, wildflower, fern and leaf as motif, or a nautical one, with a fish, boat, lighthouse and the like. Or use a garden flower or a geometric design, or a handsome monogram.

When you finish hooking a mat or coaster, trim the backing to about ½ inch from the outside row of loops. Turn this edge under and fasten it down with basting stitches. Then, cut a piece of felt to the exact size and shape of the piece, place this on the back and fasten the edges of the felt and mat together with close overcast stitches. Stitches tend to be buried in the two materials and so are not visible at the edges.

DOORSTOPS

Covered bricks make wonderful doorstops and are welcomed as gifts. You can plan a design with a recipient in mind. For a child, a bright rocking horse, a kitten or puppy; a fish or boat for a sailor, a handsome eagle for the antique lover or a rose for the gardener. Vivid colors and all-over designs can be used for making very stylish doorstops.

To make a covered brick doorstop, draw or purchase a pattern that is just the size of the top of a brick. After hooking, trim the backing to about 1 inch from the outside of the loops. Then wrap the brick with a piece of scrap material from your sewing basket or with paper towels, to pad rough edges and keep them from rubbing through the cover.

Now, fasten the hooked piece to the brick with Scotch tape. This will hold the raw edges of backing down. Use felt or flannel to make a "box" to cover the sides and bottom of the brick, choosing a color that goes well with the background hue of the design.

For the box, place the brick on the material and cut a rectangular piece, large enough so that the sides can be brought up to the edge of the pattern. Make square corners, whipstitching the seams and then trim off the excess material. Pull the box on over the brick and fasten the top edge of the fabric to the outside row of loops of the design. Stitch from the edge of the fabric up through the loops with close overcasting. The stitches will be buried and will not show.

With mats, coasters and doorstops, if you plan to make several, work in assembly-line fashion. Draw a number of designs on a single piece of backing, and mount the backing on a frame. Finish all designs before cutting them out.

HOOKING TO SELL

A discussion of small hooked articles leads naturally to a discussion of hooking to sell. Small pieces can be completed rather quickly and so can be offered for a relatively small price. Also, they can be made in a variety of designs and colors to suit different tastes.

You can arrange to sell your work by advertising in your local newspaper with your home serving as a shop. Usually, it is better to display your work in a store as the articles will be seen by more people. Gift, hobby or other specialty shops are quite willing to show small unusual articles that are appealing and attractive. You can arrange with the owner to market them on a commission basis or sell articles directly to him.

Prepare several sample pieces to show, taking care that these cover a range of design and color. Forget your own preferences in the beginning. Once you build up a reputation for your work, you can afford to specialize in the style you prefer, whether it is realistic, shaded hooking or abstract, modern design. It is relatively easy to sell small hooked articles, providing they show imagination in design and color and are of meticulous workmanship. But selling hooked rugs is another matter. This is bigger business and so requires more careful planning.

As a rule, it is wiser to sell rugs on a custom-made basis than to make several and then try to market them. Of course, with rugs as with small articles, you would have to show samples of your work before taking orders. But by taking orders for specific patterns, with an idea of the colors preferred, you avoid working for many weeks on a rug that may wait a long time for a customer. Also, by taking orders, you can set the price in advance, deciding on one that is satisfactory to you and to the buyer.

However, if you have made many rugs

and wish to sell some of them, you can do so either by advertising or by placing them in a shop. Sell them directly or arrange for a commission. If you have reproduced primitive rugs, antique shops are a good place to display your work. If your rugs are bold in design and color, show them in stores that specialize in modern furnishings.

Hooking to sell can be a lucrative business. Income will depend, of course, on wisdom in planning and the amount of time and effort expended. But even if you sell only a few articles, you will derive the satisfaction that everyone receives from knowing they can make something that is valued by others. This pleasure is quite aside from the amount of money involved and can serve as a real booster to morale.

CHAPTER 13

Teaching the Craft

How Can I Become a Teacher?

THE best way to share your skill is by teaching others how to hook. There is a real need for qualified teachers of the craft and rewards for teaching are multiple and varied. The most obvious reward is financial, and many people have found teaching either a means of livelihood or a way to earn extra money. Less apparent, but equally rewarding, are the personal satisfactions gained from sharing—the increase in confidence, the knowledge of usefulness and an enlarged understanding of oneself and of others.

The greatest reward of all can come in a special area of teaching, the field of occupational therapy. Here you can help those who are in genuine need of absorbing, creative work. Indeed, your teaching can make the difference between hope and despair for a mental patient, an elderly person, an invalid or one who is partially disabled.

THE ROAD TO TEACHING

At this moment, you may be quite unable to imagine yourself teaching others how to hook. Perhaps you cannot envision a time when you will feel adequately prepared with either technical knowledge or stamina. In fact, you may not believe that you will ever want to teach.

However, many people who are now successful teachers have had these same doubts, and quite a number have started teaching, not because of a definite decision to do so, but through a natural course of events. There is a well-trodden road to teaching that has been followed so often that you, too, may follow it—and long before you feel you know everything about the craft.

You take the first step on this road when you teach a friend how to hook. As

I have already remarked, friends and neighbors will be interested in your hobby and want to learn all you can tell them about it. Since there are not enough professional rug-hooking teachers to go around, you will be called on by increasing numbers of people as word spreads.

At first, you may just demonstrate technique, but eventually, perhaps right after you have learned, you will be showing a few friends how to dye. You may postpone this instruction for a while by sharing your own dyed material, but there is a limit to this. Besides, sooner or later, someone will want a color that you do not happen to have.

While you are instructing in technique and dyeing, you will be talking about design and color. Each time you discuss these, your ideas will be developed and clarified so that you will present them more effectively to the next group of interested beginners. There will be successive groups, I promise you, and if you love your hobby, it will be difficult to say no to anyone who wants to learn. As a result, your own time to enjoy the craft may become increasingly limited and you will maneuver to try to help yourself as well as others. Perhaps you will arrange to have all those who are interested come to your home at a definite time. But what about those who telephone or just drop in, asking only to see the rug you are making, to watch you work for a moment to see how it is done?

Now, in self-defense, you announce that you are teaching classes in rug hooking, with a scheduled series of lessons on a paying basis. You have reached the end of the road. This is not a bad road to teaching, even though it may seem a back

one, and, of course, you may start teaching some other way. Some hookers have prepared to teach right from the beginning, while others have started as the result of a need to earn money due to a change in financial circumstances or because of a desire for absorbing work. The really important thing, of course, is to be a good teacher, no matter what route you follow.

THE GOOD TEACHER ACTS AS GUIDE

I think that those who start teaching with feelings of inadequacy can sometimes provide better instruction than those who feel well prepared. For rugwork is creative and self-expression can be stifled by authority. In fact, from my viewpoint, qualities of character are at least as important as knowledge of technique, color and design.

Of course, a teacher should be familiar with basic techniques. Beyond this, it is far better to know a little about all possibilities in the craft than a lot about one particular phase. If you specialize, you may tend to insist that pupils follow your preference and infer that other directions are not worth while. While most beginners accept this type of instruction at first, some are sure to reach a point where their ideas are in opposition to a teacher's.

So, to be a good teacher, determine to act as a guide, not God, to your pupils. Lead each to a development of his own ideas, for only in this way will any individual find permanent satisfaction in creative work. To be an expert guide you will need certain qualities, for what you are can be more important to pupils than what you know. Ask yourself a few questions on this score.

Can you be patient? Beginners do not learn with the same degree of rapidity, nor do they progress with equal speed. Some absorb information quickly and are eager to learn more, while others can only take in a certain amount of instruction at one time. You must be prepared to repeat, perhaps many times, to one or two of your pupils, giving them extra time.

Are you understanding and tactful? In creative work, personality traits are revealed quickly. By recognizing these, you can encourage and praise a timid pupil, disregarding the initial quality of her work, and you can help the over-bold also, by suggesting boundaries within which she can create most effectively.

Most important, are you humble? Can you admit uncertainty about some areas in the craft, and can you realize that your preferences in color and design are not necessarily right for another? Only if you can, will you be able to be honestly enthusiastic about someone else's choice, and prepared also to encourage talent beyond your own in a pupil.

LOGICAL PROGRESSION OF LESSONS

After making some high resolves, the next step is organization. Plan a series of lessons that progress in logical fashion and that cover the possibilities of the craft. Right from the start, give pupils every chance to express preferences.

First, present and demonstrate all types of frames and hooks, giving time at end of the lesson for each person to try them out. Now, offer catalogues of several different designers and also specific information and encouragement on drawing one's own patterns. Finally, during the first lesson prepare the student for the second lesson, the use of color in rugs, perhaps by showing a few finished rugs or some color slides. Usually, this is all anyone can absorb for a first lesson.

Give the class a little time between the first and second lesson, to consider the choice of equipment, to plan or order a design, to start thinking about color and to discuss ideas at home. Allow at least a week for mulling, and you may be sure nearly all will return full of ideas and well charged with excitement.

This second meeting is an excellent time to give basic information on color. All are eager now to make a decision on color and are ready to receive instruction on principles in order to choose wisely. As a working knowledge of color is so essential in rug-work, an entire lesson can be spent on the subject. When you describe relationships of color, show specific examples whenever possible. Try to get each person to decide on a scheme and promise, for the next lesson, a demonstration of how to get any desired color by dyeing.

The third lesson is held in the kitchen, a lesson in dyeing. Move slowly through the dyeing procedure, emphasizing the relationships of color as discussed in the previous lesson. First, dye shades of one color, then show how one hue is changed by the addition of another color. Finally, demonstrate the use of several dyes of different colors mixed to obtain a single hue.

Usually, beginners are astonished by the magic of the home dye-pot. Sometimes they are astonished to the point that they are unable to remember just how it was done. For this reason, and because dyeing colors at home appears to be a real hurdle for many, type out the instruction sheets for each pupil, describing exactly the steps you followed during the dyeing demonstration. Emphasize the importance of dyeing colors in their own homes as soon as possible after they have seen you do it. Point out, also, that if they dye at least one of the colors for their rug, between now and the next lesson, they will be ready to start work. This is the goal toward which all are now striving.

Lesson four arrives, and if all goes well everyone is prepared with equipment, design and colored material, and has been practicing the hooking technique at home. This is the perfect time to discuss technique, the making of even, properly packed loops. Let them practice on the rug they plan to make, one they are anxious to have look nice. This results in care and attention to detail, and the effort is made more enjoyable by the knowledge that a well-hooked area is an actual step toward a finished rug.

Now that pupils have the preferred tool in hand, they are ready to follow a discussion of special techniques, such as shading. Some will be intensely interested in fine shading, others may not be especially keen about this kind of hooking. So, once again, emphasize principles, so that everyone will grasp the *idea* of shading, yet it will not be necessary to spend several lessons on this one phase of rug-making.

Thus you will be fair to all, not holding up those who do not care for realistic work, yet being sure that everyone knows how it is done. Hookers change direction sometimes, and those who do not want to shade now may want to in the future, while "realists" of the moment may want someday to do work in varied texture. That is why it is so important that all techniques be described and demonstrated at the start.

INDIVIDUAL HELP

Once all basic information has been given and pupils are aware of the possibilities in the craft, once they have chosen a technique, design and colors, you may feel your major task is done. Quite the contrary, for from this time on you will be giving individual help, and all your resources will be needed. As you move from frame to frame, each pupil will ask something different of you. One will not have understood how to shade, and you must patiently repeat information on this subject. Another will still be struggling to make an even row of loops, and you must give her special attention so that she will not be discouraged by the

23. PRIMITIVE FLOWER
30 by 64 inches

Hall-Prescott-Burnham Design

The primitive flowers in this design are worked in brilliant reds and yellows, the leaves are in shades of green and the background is a soft blue. Use of these colors, often associated with Pennsylvania Dutch art, makes it a dramatic, decorative rug.

more rapid progress of some of her class-mates. Still another is hooking evenly but insists that the work is not good enough. You must suggest relaxation for this perfectionist and help her realize that design and color are the really important factors in the craft.

You may find someone in the class who is starting work on a pattern given her by a friend or perhaps one suggested by her family. If she is approaching the work with little enthusiasm, point out that a rug is a long-term project, both in execution and years of use, so that it is doubly foolish to begin on any pattern that is not personally appealing. In any class, you will also find one or two who are afraid to express themselves despite the encouragement you have given. Affirm again that all are able to create and gently but firmly push them from dependence on you or a classmate.

These are problems sometimes found in teaching a group of women. When working with either elderly people or children, some of these are accentuated while others are not so apparent. With both old and young, lessons must be slow and easy as the attention span of these age groups is short. Also, older people generally require more encouragement to express themselves, but youngsters are usually quite uninhibited and will move rapidly to original work in both design and color.

JOYS OF TEACHING

I have mentioned a few of the problems in teaching only so that you will be prepared for them and not be discouraged should they arise. For, in truth, the joys of teaching far outnumber the sorrows. Guide your pupils with a sure but delicate hand and you will certainly find several who have listened attentively and have gone to work to draw an original, beautiful design. Others will have succeeded in dyeing exquisite colors for a scheme that will inspire you as well as other members of the class. Also, you will have gifted pupils, those whose ideas, enthusiasm or personality are stimulating to everyone.

In fact, after working together for only a short time, as each member of the class begins to find satisfaction in expressing herself, she will be concerned to help those around her. Pupils can learn much from one another, and this makes your task easier. You, too, will learn from those you teach and best of all, you will find that the base of mutual concern in creative work is excellent for forming close, lasting friendships.

THE GREATEST REWARD

The greatest reward in teaching can come from using your knowledge to meet a genuine need, a need beyond that

24. TREE OF LIFE
38 by 50 inches

Designed by Charlotte Stratton   *Hooked by Karl A. Larsen*

Mr. Larsen hooked this delightful pattern when he was eighty years old. The workmanship is meticulous, and the colors delicately shaded in a realistic treatment. It makes a decorative wall hanging in his daughter's home.

TREE OF LIFE

of the usual hooking class. There are those to whom creative work can actually mean the difference between complete apathy and aroused interest in themselves and in others. These are people in institutions, in rest homes and hospitals.

In sharing your hobby with friends or in teaching, you will encounter individuals who are lonely or lack confidence. By offering companionship and by teaching a skill, you will help these people and will find special satisfaction in knowing that you have done so.

HELP FOR MENTAL PATIENTS

With many of the patients in mental hospitals, feelings of inadequacy differ only in degree to those that we all feel. They differ to a point where patients simply withdraw rather than try to cope with the problems of life. Those who are withdrawn or disturbed can be helped by occupational therapy, by introduction to work that is absorbing enough to lessen concentration on self. A creative pastime can provide an escape from a dark, inner world and make possible the first step toward awareness of others. Increased awareness of others can lead to association with an individual or a group, the next step toward the goal toward which many mental patients strive—return to a normal way of life.

Rug-hooking has already proved valuable in several mental hospitals. In one, the Grafton State Hospital, at North Grafton, Massachusetts, an occupational therapist, Madeleine Davis, sums up its values for patients in this way:

"Rug-hooking appeals to the love of color; there is association with rugs as a part of the preparation to return to their homes. Through this work, patients can make gifts suitable for friends or relatives, and it can provide relaxation and freedom from idleness or noise and be a means of funds to help prepare for rehabilitation."

One of Mrs. Davis's patients, a grandmother, makes an especially touching tribute to hooking by saying, "For the first time in ten years I have a gift for my daughter and grandson that I'm not ashamed to send at Christmas." Illustration 23 shows a rug hooked by a patient in a mental hospital.

ELDERLY PEOPLE, INVALIDS AND THE PHYSICALLY HANDICAPPED

Rug-work can bring satisfaction to old people, invalids and to the physically handicapped, as well as to mental patients. These people want something to do and need an absorbing occupation. Further, they need to feel they are contributing for otherwise they lose self-respect and its accompaniments—dignity and hope.

For some, the ability to make something that will provide even a small income can bring the important sense of independence. For others, a hobby can be a link with others, a longed-for opportunity to make friends. To both the elder citizens who made the rugs shown in Illustrations 24 and 25, the craft has brought these things.

For many, hooking can even help physically. This is especially true for victims of arthritis, as the technique has been found to keep fingers from stiffening and to strengthen hand and arm muscles.

Dr. Ruth Brenner, of Manheim, Penn-

25. FOREST AND GARDEN
43 by 52 inches

Heirloom Design   *Hooked by Olive B. Russell*

Mrs. Russell has been making hooked rugs for over thirty years, finding it a
never ending source of satisfaction and pleasure and a fine way to make friends.
She has worked the roses on this rug in shades ranging from pale pink to wine
on a background of warm beige and has used deep brown in the wide border
with touches of the same brown in the pine cones.

sylvania, has used the craft for many of
her patients, among whom are those with
arthritis, heart conditions, multiple scle-
rosis, fractured hips and even bilateral
cataracts. It is evident from the comments
of those whom she has instructed that
physically handicapped people welcome
an opportunity to work. Once given the
knowledge, they themselves will provide
both ingenuity and courage.

A fine example of this is shown by
Mrs. Draper Buch, one of Dr. Brenner's
patients who is a victim of multiple scle-

rosis. Although she must wear a neck
brace and can only work for short periods,
she has been hooking for ten years, and
says, "I often wonder what I would have
been like if Dr. Brenner hadn't started me
on hooking. I'd have had nothing to do,
shut in for ten years with just an occasional outing in the car, and it would have
been a miserable existence. Through my
hobby, I have made many wonderful
friends and it has given me something to
talk about. Being a woman, I love to do
that. I hope that other folks who need

26. VARIETY
2 by 3 feet

Designed by Charlotte Stratton   *Hooked by Janet Buch*

Mrs. Buch has been hooking for ten years, despite difficulties that would discourage many people. She feels that others like herself will find rug-making a rewarding, absorbing hobby. The attractive scattered design on this half-round is delicately shaded, the leaves in olive and bronze greens and the border in shades of bronze gold. And the background is a deep hue of American Beauty red.

therapy will get started on hooking and find out for themselves what a wonderful, worthwhile art it is."

I think you will agree that Mrs. Buch shows both courage and determination, and I am sure you will agree that her work is beautiful as it appears in Illustration 26.

THE RIGHT SPIRIT

If you have the qualities needed for teaching people in your community, you also have all that is required for sharing your skill with those whose need is so great. By this sharing, you will receive more than you give, especially if you approach the task in a spirit of real interest, not with conscious charity. Doctors, nurses and internes in hospitals, owners and managers of rest homes—all welcome anything that will help their patients. Make your offer of help specific by getting together enough equipment, material and patterns to enable a few patients

27. WHIMSEY
34 by 63 inches

Designed by Pearl McGown   *Hooked by Daisy Short*

This lovely rug is one of several that Daisy Short has made since she became blind. She finds great satisfaction and pleasure in hooking and is delighted that others can see the results. Her daughter helped her select and place colors in this design, with leaf shadings from pale pink to deep wine and touches of green to brighten them. The background is an attractive combination of beige and gray tweeds.

to start work. Usually this is all that is necessary to begin with for as more patients become interested, hospital funds will be available to purchase supplies.

To stimulate interest, bring a few small, finished pieces to show. Bring a scrapbook also, with pictures that suggest ideas for rugs. Sometimes, a patient who does not want to hook will enjoy working on the scrapbook. Another may help prepare material, thus assisting the hookers and benefiting herself as well by her opportunity to contribute.

It is important to encourage patients to grasp every opportunity for interest that the craft offers, to select colors and a design that she likes and to draw her own pattern if she wishes. Further, she should be assured that her work is entirely her own, a gratifying expression of her individuality.

AN OPEN DOOR

I received the rug shown in Illustration 27 from Mrs. Lydia Hicks of Syracuse, New York, with the information that it was hooked, under her tutelage, by a woman who is blind.

As you can see, the design is attractive, and I assure you that both workmanship and color are excellent. It is in every way a beautiful hooked piece.

I am certain that the craft would be as satisfying and absorbing for those who are blind as it is for many other workers. I am sure, too, that finished articles as nicely done as the rug pictured could be sold readily, providing a fine source of income. It is apparent that one sightless individual, with the help of a friend, can enjoy hooking, and it remains only to devise a means whereby all who are similarly afflicted could find pleasure in the craft.

Texture is so much a part of hooking that one can tell, with eyes closed, whether loops are pulled up evenly and backing filled properly. The blind would be aided by their well developed tactile sense, both in learning the technique and working on a pattern. The only real difficulty would arise in following outlines of design and in selecting colors. This could be surmounted by means of a specially prepared rug kit, with lines and areas of design and bags of separate colors marked so they could be identified by touch.

As far as I know, the door to the profit and pleasure found in rug hooking has not been fully opened to those who cannot see. May I suggest that just a little effort is required to open it and that the dedicated person who does so will be assured of the great happiness that comes from service to others.

CHAPTER 14

All About Speed Hooking

I HAVE already described the relaxed, peaceful feeling that comes from using a hand hook. It is this that makes it the ideal tool for those who prefer working at a slow, precise pace. A hand hook is also the perfect tool for the no-hurry times we all have when it is pleasant to have a project that we know will take many months of slow, careful work to complete.

However, many people like to work fast, and most of us have hurry-up times when it is stimulating, or necessary, to know that a project can be completed in just a few weeks. A speed hook is the perfect tool for those temperaments, and those times, that require speed.

After a small amount of practice with a speed hook, you can easily fill a square foot of background in an hour, an area that would take four or five hours to fill using a hand hook. This means that you can complete a good-sized rug—a 3- by 5-foot rug for example—in a little more than a week, hooking for just two hours a day. Furthermore, the rug you make with a speed hook can be as beautiful and as durable as a rug made with a hand hook.

THE APPEAL OF SPEED

Young people—children, teen-agers, and young homemakers—usually prefer a simple technique that produces results quickly. Elderly people also like a project that is easy and doesn't take so long that it becomes either boring or discouraging. And speed hooking gives those in the middle years, busy mothers and career women, the opportunity to make a hooked rug in the few spare hours they have available for a hobby.

Speed hooking is well suited to men also, not only because they like the rapidity with which a rug can be completed but also because they enjoy the strong hand action required by the speed hook; it gives a satisfying feeling of production.

Everyone enjoys watching the design

of a rug taking shape and noticing how the colors go together. The speed hook provides the excitement of seeing these things quickly, plus the pleasure of knowing that it will be possible to try out many ideas for design and color by making many rugs.

In addition, while we all cherish the knowledge that the rugs we make will last for many years to give pleasure to future generations, most of us would like to enjoy our rugs longer ourselves and completing them quickly gives us this chance.

PRACTICAL ADVANTAGES OF SPEED

A speed hook offers definite advantages to those of you who are furnishing your first home or redecorating your home extensively. You can actually plan a schedule of rug making—two small rugs for the living room, to be completed in October; one rug for each bedroom, to be completed in November.

By planning all the rugs for your home at one time, you can avoid "patchwork" decorating because, right at the start, you can plan a related scheme in the design and colors of the rugs to be used in the same room, or of rugs to be used throughout your home.

A speed hook can also help you realize the ambition of many ardent rug hookers, which is to make a room-sized rug. Beyond the feeling of personal triumph this will bring, you will find that both the decorative impact of the rug, and the admiration of friends will probably be in direct proportion to the size of your rug. Husbands are particularly impressed by a large rug when they realize that you have covered wide areas

of floor without spending hundreds of dollars at a carpet store.

With a speed hook, you can make rugs that you can give away without inward pangs, for it isn't nearly as difficult to part with a rug that has taken a few weeks to make as it is to part with one that has taken many months.

Finally, if you want to produce hooked rugs to sell and expect to realize a proper return for the time you spend making them, it is good business to make these rugs in as little time as possible.

TWO KINDS OF SPEED HOOKS

All speed hooks do just what hand hooks do, but they do it in a different way. Like the hand hook, the speed hook fills the mesh of a rug foundation fabric with loops of yarn or cloth. However, the speed hook *pushes* the yarn or cloth from the *top side* of the foundation fabric into loops on the *under side*. The hand hook *lifts* the yarn or cloth from the *under side* of the foundation fabric into loops on the *top side*.

Thus, when you are using a speed hook, you will need to look underneath your work surface to see the eventual surface of your rug.

There are two basic kinds of speed hooks. One kind takes both hands to operate; the other kind requires only one hand. There are several speed hooks of both kinds on the market and I have made an effort to try most of them to determine which ones are the easiest to use and the most versatile.

Two-handed speed hooks, like the Susan Burr (see page 44) have a handle that is divided in the center to allow one side of the handle to be pushed forward by one hand while the other side is drawn back by the other hand. This back-and-forth motion of the handle pushes the needle tip of the tool through the foundation fabric, setting loops on the reverse side of this fabric.

These two-handed speed hooks are easy to learn to use, they can be threaded with either yarn or strips of cloth, and they have an arrangement for making loops of various heights.

However, the arm-shoulder motion required to operate these hooks does not permit precise control of where each loop is placed. Therefore, this kind of speed hook is best suited to designs where there are no intricate, small areas to be filled, or to filling background areas.

The Columbia-Minerva Deluxe Punch Needle is a one-handed speed hook. Learning to use this tool is also easy, and the wrist motion required to operate it provides very good control of where each loop is placed. Thus, this tool can be used effectively to hook designs with small areas and it can be used also to fill large areas rapidly.

This speed hook has settings to enable you to make ten different loop heights, from a low ¼-inch loop to a ⅞-inch loop.

The Columbia-Minerva Punch Needle can be threaded with either yarn or strips of cloth, but it is much more easily threaded with yarn. Considerable tension must be applied to the material that is being threaded to force it into the narrow slot in the handle of this tool. Strips of cloth that are narrow enough to go through the eye of the needle tip of the tool tend to break under this tension.

However, yarn has special advantages over strips of cloth for speed hooking.

Cloth strips are usually in rather short lengths, making it necessary to stop work and rethread the speed hook frequently. Since yarn can be continuously reeled, it is only necessary to rethread the hook when you have finished a ball of yarn or want to change to another color.

The Columbia-Minerva Punch Needle used with yarn, therefore, provides the easiest and fastest way to hook every type of rug design. Step-by-step instructions for using this tool are included in this chapter.

I have not mentioned the latch hook in this discussion of different kinds of speed hooks, although many people think of it as a speed tool for rug hooking. The latch hook is actually a tool for making knotted rugs, with a device near the tip of the tool that ties short, cut pieces of yarn into a stiff, open-mesh canvas.

This is quite unlike the loop-placing technique used in making hooked rugs, and a rug made with a latch hook is quite unlike one made with either a hand hook or one of the speed hooks I have just described. Because the latch-hook rug uses cut pieces of yarn, it has a shag surface and the design is blurred, while the short, uncut loops that are most characteristic of the true rug hooking technique produce clear design edges and a flat, even surface that is more durable and easier to clean than a shag surface.

FOUNDATION FABRIC FOR SPEED HOOKING

Speed hooks require an especially strong, pliable foundation fabric and of the two fabrics used for rug hooking, burlap and monk's cloth, the latter is preferable.

There are various kinds of monk's cloth available, ranging from a lightweight, open-weave kind frequently sold as drapery fabric, to a stiff, very heavy cloth sometimes used for rug hooking. However, the best monk's cloth for speed hooking is a medium-weight, soft, two-ply cotton. This material is pliable enough so that the threads separate readily to allow easy entry of the needle tip of the speed hook and yet it is strong enough to take the strong thrust of the speed hook against its surface without fear of breaking threads.

THE BEST FRAME

For the same reasons that speed hooking requires a strong fabric, it requires a strong frame. The frame must be sturdy enough to permit the foundation fabric to be very tightly stretched to provide a resistant surface to the thrust of the speed hook. And the frame must provide a means of *keeping* the foundation fabric taut despite the repeated push of the speed hook against the fabric.

The hoop frames that are adequate for use with a hand hook will not serve when using a speed hook. The foundation fabric will sag at the first thrust of the speed hook because the cloth is merely held between the bands of the hoop. Fastening the fabric to the bars of a frame with thumb tacks does not work well either as the tacks tend to pop out. Although the foundation fabric can be laced to the bars of a frame, or secured with carpet tacks, these are tedious, time-consuming procedures and do not permit quick re-tightening of the fabric.

I have devised the following method of mounting the foundation fabric on a frame to insure that it will stay taut and also make it possible to remove the fabric from the frame quickly and restretch it to work on different sections of the design. In addition, with this stretching method, it is possible to make a large rug on a rather small frame.

I use a Bliss Adjustable Frame (this is the same as the Fraser Standing Frame) in the 20-inch size, and I place finishing nails, a 1-inch size, along all four bars of this frame, about 2 inches apart. I stretch the rug pattern tight and straight on these nails just as one would stretch a curtain on a curtain stretcher. When I have hooked the section of the pattern that is within the stretched area, I simply lift the pattern off the nails and restretch it on again to hook another section. The very small heads of the finishing nails slip up easily through the mesh of the foundation fabric and also slide easily between the loops of an already-worked section of the pattern.

You can use this mounting method on a home-made frame if you wish. Four lengths of wood, secured at the corners to keep them aligned, are all that are needed. Canvas stretchers, available at art supply stores, can also be used to make a frame for speed hooking. It makes hooking easier, of course, if you use a frame with legs. Otherwise, it is necessary to have the bottom edge of your frame resting on your lap and the top edge placed against a table.

With this finishing-nail mounting method, the size of the frame does not limit the size of the rug pattern to be mounted on it. The part of the pattern that is not stretched within the area of the four bars of the frame simply hangs down from the back and sides of the frame. While this does not look as tidy as a pattern laced within the area of the frame, with the worked section neatly rolled under, it makes it possible to do a large rug on a small frame and also to see every section of the rug pattern at a glance.

YARNS FOR SPEED HOOKING

My initial enthusiasm for using all kinds of material for hooked rugs has been tempered over the years as I have noted the difference in durability and ease of cleaning between one kind of material and another.

Cotton material, whether yarn or cloth, does not wear as well as wool and is difficult to keep clean. The ideal yarn for speed hooking is either 100 per cent wool or a combination of wool and one of the synthetic materials. This kind of yarn will have a springy quality that gives a luxurious look and feel to a rug, it will be dirt-resistant and easy to clean, and it will be extremely durable. Furthermore, the elasticity of this kind of yarn makes placing the loops easier and causes the loops to spread out readily to cover the surface of the rug.

Not surprisingly, the best quality yarn is usually the most expensive. But, frankly, I buy the best available yarn for my rug hooking while practicing frugality in other areas of my life. I reason that all the planning and effort that go into making a hooked rug, even though it is made in just a week's time with a speed hook, warrant using the very best material.

You can choose from many different weights of yarn. Heavy rug yarn will give luxurious thickness to a hooked rug and also help to fill the foundation fabric rapidly. Lightweight yarn produces a tapestry-like effect, a rug that resembles needlepoint and is light enough to use as a wall hanging.

You can employ different weights of yarn in a single rug to obtain special effects. You can also use different loop heights for this, achieving a sculptured effect by hooking part of the design in high loops and part in low loops. You can create interesting effects by cutting some of the loops and leaving some loops uncut.

Bear in mind, however, that the handsomest hooked rugs usually feature only one thing—the texture, the color, or the design. Too many prima donnas can spoil the show. If texture is to be featured— the drama of very high loops, for example —it is usually best to keep the design and color subordinate.

Generally, I like to have the design of a rug as its main feature, with color serving mainly to complement the particular kind of design. To permit the design to show clearly, I use low loops, all of the same height, and I leave them uncut. Using low loops has other advantages too. They are less expensive since they use less yarn. They are easier to keep clean, and not as likely as long loops to be pulled out by pets or to catch ladies by the heels.

HOOKING WITH THE COLUMBIA-MINERVA PUNCH NEEDLE

The Columbia-Minerva Punch Needle has two needle points. The larger one is for use with heavy yarn, the smaller one for use with lightweight yarn. To begin, insert the needle point that is appropriate to the yarn you are using into the handle of the punch needle. Push this point up through the handle to the slot which determines the loop height, then click it into place by twisting it to the left.

Roll your yarn into a ball so it can run through the needle in a continuous strand. Thread the yarn through the metal circle at one end of the needle and then down through the eye of the needle. See-saw the yarn back and forth gently, holding it taut, to ease it into the hollow slot in the handle, as shown in Figure 20. Leave about an inch of yarn protruding from the eye of the needle.

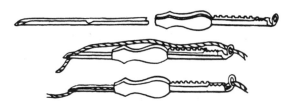

Figure 20.

Hold the needle as you would hold a pencil. Keep it at a slight slant, with the open groove of the needle up and facing in the direction in which you plan to work. Be sure the yarn is running freely. You will find that you can manipulate the needle to work in straight lines, or curving lines. It is easiest to outline a section of design first, then fill the center of this part of the design with curving rows following the outline row. To do the background, block off areas with long curving rows before filling.

Place loops close enough to cover the rug surface adequately but do not try to fill every opening in the mesh or count openings for filling. With heavy rug yarn, 4 or 5 stitches to the inch, and 5 rows to

the inch, is usually adequate. You may wish to do some practice rows to judge proper spacing between loops with the weight yarn you are using. You can pull out these practice rows and reuse the yarn, and practice will not hurt the rug backing.

Push the needle through the foundation fabric right up to the hilt, as shown in Figure 21a. Actually *hitting* the foundation fabric with the hilt of the needle insures setting loops securely all at the same height.

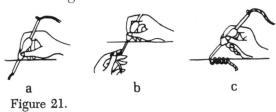

a   b   c

Figure 21.

Keep the needle inserted in the foundation fabric and reach underneath to pull the yarn down through so that about a 2-inch length is left on the under side of the foundation fabric. This procedure is shown in Figure 21b. This tag end of yarn, now on the surface of your rug, can be clipped even with the loops when you have finished a section of the rug or when you have completed the rug.

Now you are ready to place your first loop. Bring the needle back up to the top side of the foundation fabric, slide it along just slightly above the surface of this fabric, then push it through again firmly. Go slowly at first, easing the needle up and just clearing the surface of the foundation fabric between loops. If you pull the needle up too vigorously or too high above the work surface, you may pull out a few of the loops you have already set. Figure 21c shows a hand holding the needle properly, and it shows the slight angle that is most effective in moving the needle across the foundation fabric. Figure 21c also shows the first tag end of yarn below the work surface, and several loops already placed.

When you want to rethread the punch needle, leave the needle point inserted in the foundation fabric and reach underneath to clip the yarn about 1 inch from the end of the needle.

SPECIAL DESIGN & COLOR OPPORTUNITIES

With a Columbia-Minerva Punch Needle, you can fill intricate small areas of design with many shades of color to create the painted-in-wool effect that is the aim of many people when they use a hand hook.

However, you can also enjoy doing designs that are seldom attempted with a hand hook. Since filling is so rapid, you can have fun doing designs with broad areas of a single color, designs that are simply flowing areas of various colors, or that use just two colors.

When you use a speed hook, it isn't necessary to have frequent changes of color or the challenge of intricate design to keep the hooking process interesting. You are freed, by speed, to concentrate on the total, overall effect that you want rather than on the shading of a scroll, a leaf, or a petal.

Intricate design isn't always the best design, and realistically shaded rugs are not appropriate in many homes. The trend today, in fabric design, in art, and in home decoration generally, is toward bolder design, broader spread of color, and more abstract representation.

Rather than portray a subject realistically, you can elicit the *feeling* of the subject through design and color. The drama of a flower such as the anemone might be recreated in a design that had splashes of scarlet, purple, pink, and white, and touches of black, with no suggestion of an actual petal. Similarly, the airy grace of a dandelion seed head and the special feeling of early summer might be recreated by using radiating lines of very pale green against a dark green background.

George Wells' *Stained Glass*, Color Illustration XXIII, is a good example of the way in which color and design in a hooked rug can produce a special feeling. With its predominantly somber hues accented by touches of bright blue and rose, this rug offers the same startling contrast that one finds in ancient cathedrals between the brilliance of the glass and the dark stone that surrounds it.

You, too, can make a rug that recreates the feeling you have about a particular subject, or you can make a rug that portrays the subject realistically. You can make bold, bright rugs or subdued, delicate ones, trying out different kinds of design and combinations of color, to suit all your varying moods. With a speed hook, you will find that it's all fun because it's all fast.

Bibliography

BOOKS ABOUT RUG HOOKING

Allen, Edith Louise, *Rugmaking Craft*. Peoria, Illinois: Manual Arts Press, 1946.

Batchelder, Martha. *Art of Hooked Rug Making*. Peoria, Illinois: Bennett, 1947.

Bowles, Ella Shannon. *Handmade Rugs*. Boston, Massachusetts: Little Brown, 1927.

Bowles, Ella Shannon. *Homespun Handicrafts*. Philadelphia: J. B. Lippincott, 1931.

Eaton, Allen H. *Handicrafts of New England*. New York: Harper, 1949.

Hicks, Amy. *Craft of Handmade Rugs*. New York: Empire State Book Company, 1936.

Kent, William Winthrop. *The Hooked Rug*. New York: Tudor, 1937.

Kent, William Winthrop. *Rare Hooked Rugs*. Springfield, Massachusetts: Pond-Eckberg, 1941.

Kent, William Winthrop. *Hooked Rug Design*. Springfield, Massachusetts: Pond-Eckberg, 1949.

King, Mrs. Harry. *How to Hook Rugs*. Batesville, Arkansas: The Author, 1949.

Langenberg, Ella. *Stitching, Crocheting and Hooked Rug Making*. New York: Holden, 1941.

Lawless, Dorothy. *Rug Hooking and Braiding*. New York: Crowell, 1952.

McGown, Pearl. *Color in Hooked Rugs*. West Boylston, Massachusetts: The Author, 1954.

O'Brien, Mildred J. *The Rug and Carpet Book*. New York: Barrows, 1946.

Philips, A. M. L. *Hooked Rugs and How to Make Them*. New York: Macmillan, 1930.

Rex, Stella Hay. *Practical Hooked Rugs*. New York: Ziff-Davis, 1949.

Rex, Stella Hay. *Choice Hooked Rugs*. Englewood Cliffs, New Jersey: Prentice-Hall, 1953.

Ries, Estelle H. *American Rugs*. Cleveland: World Publishing Company, 1950.

SOME SOURCES OF IDEAS FOR DESIGN AND COLOR IN RUG WORK

Ashton, Pearl F. *Everyone Can Paint Fabrics*. New York: Studio Publications, 1952.

Barker, Alfred F. *Ornamentation and Textile Design*. London, England: Methuen and Company, 1930.

Chapman, Suzanne E. *Early American Design Motifs*. New York: Dover Publications, 1952.

Chase, Joseph Cummings. *Creative Design*. New York: John Wiley and Sons, 1934.

Cheskin, Louis. *Colors, What They Can Do For You*. New York: Liveright Publications Corporation, 1947.

Christensen, Irwin O. *Index of American Design* New York: Macmillan Company, 1950.

English Domestic Needlework of the XVI, XVII and XVIII Centuries. New York: The Metropolitan Museum of Art, 1945.

Guptil, Arthur L. *Color in Sketching and Rendering*. New York: Reinhold Publishing Corporation, 1949.

Hallen, Julienne. *Folk Art Designs*. New York: Homecrafts, 1949.

Hendrickson, Edwin A. *Mosaic Patterns*. New York: Hill and Wang, 1958.

Hunt, Antony. *Textile Design*. New York: Studio Publications, 1951.

119

Hungarian Decorative Folk Art. Budapest, Hungary: Hungarian Ethnographical Museum, 1955.

Jones, Owen. *The Grammar of Ornament.* London, England: Bernard Quaritch, 1928.

Kauffman, Henry. *Pennsylvania Dutch, American Folk Art.* New York: American Studio Books, 1946.

Katzenbach, Lois and William. *The Practical Book of American Wallpaper.* Philadelphia, Pennsylvania: J. P. Lippincott Company, 1951.

Murray, Maria D. *The Art of Tray Painting.* New York: Studio Publications, 1954.

Peto, Florence. *American Quilts and Coverlets.* New York: Chanticleer Press, 1949.

Pettit, Florence Harvey. *Block Printing on Fabrics.* New York: Hastings House, 1952.

Robertson, Elizabeth Wells. *American Quilts.* New York: Studio Publications, 1948.

Smith, Janet K. *A Manual of Design.* New York: Reinhold Publishing Corporation, 1950.

Waring, Janet. *Early American Stencils.* New York: William R. Scott, 1937.

Suppliers

WOOLEN MATERIAL

Carlbert Rug Supplies (also pre-cut material)
P.O. Box 84
Portland, Maine

Brooks
South Harwich
Massachusetts

Rovner's
Center Street
Dennisport, Massachusetts

Rivkin Remnant Store
22 Woodward Avenue
South Norwalk, Connecticut

Mrs. Hall Taylor
Whisconier Hill
Brookfield, Connecticut

North Star Woolen Mill Company
Lima, Ohio

Wool Remnant Company
P.O. Box 181
New York 13, New York

RUG YARN (* also equipment, backing, patterns and dyes)

Yarn International
P.O. Box 123
Islip, Long Island
New York

Grant Hand Weaving Supply Company
295 West 1st North
Provo, Utah

* George Wells
Cedar Swamp Road
Glen Head, Long Island
New York

* Dorothy Flick Industries
5900 Northwest Highway
Chicago 31, Illinois

* Dorothy Flick Industries
3034 North Glendale Boulevard
Los Angeles 39, California

* John E. Garrett Limited
New Glasgow, Nova Scotia

* Paternayan Brothers
312 East 95th Street
New York 28, New York

Heritage Hill Patterns
c/o Barbara Zarbock
Box 624, Westport, Connecticut

Clifford Hotchkiss
Rug Design Studio
Black Mountain, North Carolina

William Condon and Sons
65 Queen Street
Charlottetown, Prince Edward Island

EQUIPMENT

Berry's of Maine
Cumberland Center, Maine

Harry M. Fraser (also patterns and swatches)
192 Hartford Road
Manchester, Connecticut

Ralph Hylan (also swatches)
119 Pleasant Street
Arlington, Massachusetts

The Handcraft Shoppe (also patterns and
    swatches)
Old King's Highway, North
Darien, Connecticut

Hook-Art Guild
Cumberland Mills, Maine

DYES (° also equipment)

° W. Cushing and Company
Dover-Foxcroft, Maine

Putnam Fadeless Dyes
Monroe Chemical Company
Quincy, Illinois

PATTERNS (° also equipment and material
    † publications, informational material
    ‡teacher)

°† Craftsman Patterns
Wilbur Associates
Box 228
Dover-Foxcroft, Maine

°†‡ Pearl K. McGown Designs
Pearl K. McGown, Inc.
West Boylston, Massachusetts

Whitney Patterns
Mattie M. Whitney
Harwich Port, Massachusetts

‡ Cape Cod Originals
Mrs. Katherine Doane
Chatham, Massachusetts

Skaket Patterns
Mrs. Clyde Mackenzie
Orleans, Massachusetts

°†‡ Charlotte Stratton Designs
Mrs. Winthrop Davis
49 Pleasant Street
Trumbull, Connecticut

°† Modern Designs (also custom designing)
George Wells
Cedar Swamp Road
Glen Head, Long Island, New York

Patterns of several designers
°‡ Mrs. Bruce Tomlinson
Stepney Depot
Monroe, Connecticut

E. Dana Designs (also custom designing)
Mrs. Newton T. Dana
196 West Norwalk Road
Darien, Connecticut

Hall-Prescott-Burnham Designs
°† Mrs. Carl F. Hall
R.F.D. #1
Portsmouth, New Hampshire

°† Mildred Sprout Patterns
Mildred Sprout
P.O. Box 631
North Hollywood, California

Heritage Hill Patterns (also custom designing)
Dolli Tingle Designs
c/o Barbara Zarbock
Box 624, Westport, Connecticut

Dorothy Lawless Patterns
°†‡ Hooker's Guild
43012 La Tijera Station
Los Angeles 43, California

Heirloom and Hookcraft Patterns
Heirloom Rugs
54 Irving Avenue
Providence, Rhode Island

Karlkraft Patterns
Hook-Art Guild
P.O. Box 57
Cumberland Mills, Maine

Canadian Designs
Susan Frances
P.O. Box 282
Terminal "A"
Toronto, Ontario

°†‡ Rittermere Farm Studios
P.O. Box 240
Vineland, Ontario

Patterns of several designers
° ‡ Mrs. Alice Beatty
1308 Watchung Avenue
Plainfield, New Jersey

° Gilmore Brothers
Department Store
Kalamazoo, Michigan

°†‡ Mrs. Harry King Designs
Mrs. Harry King
255 North 8th Street
Batesville, Arkansas

‡ Mrs. Harold Martin
R.F.D. #1, Box 18A
Chepachet, Rhode Island

‡ Mrs. Allene M. Bily
211 North Stone Avenue
La Grange, Illinois

° Alice Maynard
558 Madison Avenue
New York 22, New York

° The Cobweb Knitting Shop
16 Avery Place
Westport, Connecticut

Pearl McGown Designs
†‡ Mrs. Lydia Hicks (equipment and instructions for special dyeing method)
2607 West Genesee Street
Syracuse, New York

Index